COMMON SENSE NATION

Common Sense Nation

UNLOCKING THE FORGOTTEN POWER
OF THE AMERICAN IDEA

Robert Curry

Encounter Books *e* New York • London

First American edition published in 2015 by Encounter Books,
an activity of Encounter for Culture and Education, Inc.,
a nonprofit, tax exempt corporation.
Encounter Books website address: www.encounterbooks.com

Manufactured in the United States and printed on
acid-free paper. The paper used in this publication meets
the minimum requirements of ANSI/NISO Z39.48 1992
(R 1997) (*Permanence of Paper*).

FIRST AMERICAN EDITION

LIBRARY OF CONGRESS CATALOGING-IN-PUBLICATION DATA
Curry, Robert, 1944–
Common sense nation: unlocking the forgotten power of the American idea/
Robert Curry.
pages cm
Includes bibliographical references and index.
ISBN 978-1-59403-825-9 (hardback)—ISBN 978-1-59403-826-6 (ebook)
1. United States—Politics and government—Philosophy. 2. Founding Fathers
of the United States. 3. United States. Declaration of Independence.
4. United States. Constitution. I. Title.
JK31.C87 2015
320.973—dc23
2015017131

Dedicated to my lovely bride, Lisa, and to my many friends at the Claremont Institute, especially Charles Kadlec, Brian Kennedy, Claire Landiss, and John Marini who so generously helped me with this book.

"The Foundation of our Empire was not laid in the gloomy age of Igno-rance and Superstition, but at an epoch when the rights of mankind were better understood and more clearly defined than at any former period; the researches of the human mind after social happiness have been carried to a great extent, the treasures of knowledge . . . are laid open for our use, and their collected wisdom may be happily applied in the establishment of our forms of government."
—GEORGE WASHINGTON ON AMERICA'S FOUNDING

"The sacred rights of mankind are . . . written, as with a sunbeam, in the whole volume of human nature, by the hand of Divinity itself, and can never be erased or obscured by mortal power."
—ALEXANDER HAMILTON

"We hold these Truths to be self-evident, that all men are created equal, that they are endowed by their Creator with certain unalien-able Rights, that among these are Life, Liberty and the pursuit of Happiness."
—THOMAS JEFFERSON

"Common Sense Realism was virtually the official creed of the American Republic . . . So what was it? . . . The power of common judgment belongs to everyone, rich or poor, educated or uneducated; indeed, we exercise it every day in hundreds of ways. Of course, ordinary people make mistakes—but so do philosophers . . . On some things, however, like the existence of the real world and basic moral truths, they know they don't have to prove it. These things are . . . self-evident, meaning they are 'no sooner understood than they are believed' because they 'carry the light of truth itself.'"
—ARTHUR HERMAN

Contents

Contents

Foreword by Victor Davis Hanson

Robert Curry believes that the roots and traditions of the Founding Fathers should once again become common knowledge to contemporary Americans. These are strange times in which all too many citizens are confused about their present culture and government. Ignorance of our own past is largely the cause. A broad cluelessness also exists about how America's creation has been deliberately massaged for contemporary political purposes in ways antithetical to the views of the Founders.

In truth, present political agendas seek to remake or obliterate the American past. Even many of those who are familiar with the contours of the American Revolution and the founding of the republic, especially in academia, journalism, the arts, and politics, believe that the late eighteenth-century birth of America was either morally problematic or has—and should have—little relevance for the contemporary United States. Twenty-first-century America, then, to the degree that it is exemplary, powerful, and influential abroad, owes its good fortune more to natural luck—a huge land mass, abundant natural resources, and a large population—in the manner of, say, Brazil, China, or Russia. Even if a nation's customs and traditions do count, our history is largely the story of an establishment of white males who thrived through the oppression of minorities, women, indigenous peoples, and immigrants, and whose founding principles still can reflect those class and racial prejudices.

Curry believes that the causes for this epidemic of false knowledge are explainable by the decline of classical liberalism. It once championed the liberty and unfettered expression of the individual, but was absorbed and corrupted by modern liberalism. The latter counterfeit doctrine immodestly assumed the state's right of almost limitless power over the individual to ensure an equality of result, largely by using government capital and power to change the nature of man. In other words, the Founders' promotion of the unfettered intellect to appreciate how divinely endowed freedom is innate to the human condition gave way to a government creed embracing secularism, atheism, and agnosticism. Only the supposedly pure reason of self-appointed experts could explain all the mysteries of man's physical and spiritual existence.

Each succeeding cadre of intellectuals would render obsolete more of the Founders' stale admonitions. These later generations were the products of a technological, sophisticated, and "improved" age of rapid social, material, and ethical progress, scarcely recognizable to the reactionaries who drafted the Bill of Rights.

In contrast, Curry emphasizes three forgotten pillars upon which the American idea was birthed and nourished. One, the creators of the American ideal drew on earlier and contemporary European free-thinkers for the Declaration of Independence, the U.S. Constitution, and *The Federalist Papers*. But their particular intellectual fonts were decidedly the Scottish Enlightenment philosophers and, to a lesser extent, their counterparts in Britain—but not so much the French Enlightenment of Voltaire and Rousseau, who were hostile to religion, favored mandated equality over constitutionally protected individual liberty, and believed in the malleability of human nature.

Classical liberalism—the confidence in the individual to think and function freely apart from government coercion—was quite different than modern liberalism. The former accepted that free choice and reasoning at times might result in inequality, but assumed that society's institutions and man's nature—religion, charities, human kindness and brotherhood—were the correctives of a humane society. Modern liberalism, in contrast—especially under Woodrow Wilson and Franklin Delano Roosevelt—did not trust either the intelligence or the maturity of the individual citizen. Modern liberals instead assumed that only properly coached and powerful elites and their technocrats could curb unhelpful personal expression and misguided individual choices to achieve more cosmic goals of equality and perceived collective fairness.

Second, a key American virtue was common sense realism, but not what later became known as intellectual pragmatism. Left to their own, largely agrarian families, self-reliant and autonomous, would bring their first-hand knowledge of nature, hard work, and human fallibility to participate in consensual government. In other words, their common sense knew well what men were and were not capable of. Basic truths of human nature and the building blocks of society were "self-evident" to the vast majority of citizens of all classes and backgrounds. Early Americans, both the public and their architects of the American system, were not late nineteenth-century utopians. They were not willing to embrace any convenient or popular creed if it supposedly offered some short-term utility in the real world—especially if it were antithetical to centuries-old intellectual, religious, and practical canons about the innate forces that motivate and admonish people.

Third, Curry assumes that the Founders are so often ignored not just because they supposedly represent a particular ossified cadre of old white privileged males, but also because their wise advice and sternness are unpalatable to the modern age of growing government. They now appear bothersome scolds and absolutists that are unhelpful for state guided and relativist social progress. The danger to personal freedom arises not just from clearly identifiable totalitarian and barbaric ideologies like Adolf Hitler's National Socialism or Joseph Stalin's communist super state. Rather, the avatars of all-encompassing government are far more insidious and subtle in assuring always increasing state services and support, and more compassionate and egalitarian group think—in exchange for the individual's surrender of inconvenient rights of free thought, obstreperous speech, and obstructive independence as envisioned by the Founders.

Finally, Citizen Curry does not offer an academic review of the origins of the American experiment. Rather, he writes and cites primary sources in an easily accessible way, offering a handbook designed, as he says, to appeal to the proverbial average citizen. Given that neither the schools nor the media, in disinterested fashion, teach us the history and purpose of America's founding and guiding principles, it remains the duty of citizens like Robert

Curry, the writer, and we the readers, jointly to rediscover who we were and are—and how we once again can become the Americans that the Founders once envisioned.

Victor Davis Hanson
Martin and Illie Anderson Senior Fellow
The Hoover Institution, Stanford University

Preface

WHY YOU WANT TO READ THIS BOOK

"We hold these Truths to be self-evident, that all men are created equal, that they are endowed by their Creator with certain unalienable Rights, that among these are Life, Liberty and the pursuit of Happiness."

We have heard and read this sentence all our lives. It is perfectly familiar. But if we pause long enough to ask ourselves why Jefferson wrote it in exactly this way, questions quickly arise.

Jefferson chose to use rather special and very precise terms. He did not simply claim that we have these rights; he claimed they are unalienable. Why "unalienable"? Unalienable, of course, means not alienable. Why was the distinction between alienable and unalienable rights so important to the Founders that it made its way into the Declaration? For that matter, where did it come from? You might almost get the impression that the Founders' examination of our rights had focused on alienable versus unalienable rights—and you would be correct.

In addition, the Declaration does not simply claim that these are truths; it claims they are self-evident truths. Why "self-evident"?

The Declaration's special claim about its truths, it turns out, is the result of those same deliberations as a result of which, in the words of George Washington, "the rights of mankind were better understood and more clearly defined than at any former period."

If a friendly visitor from another country sat you down and asked you with sincere interest why the Declaration highlights these very special terms and where they came from, could you answer clearly and accurately and with confidence? That friendly request for answers would I believe be challenging for most of us for the simple reason that we no longer conduct our politics in the language of the Founders. We simply no longer think politically in those terms. Except for ritual observances on special occasions, "unalienable rights" and "self-evident truths" have gone missing from American politics. Though familiar in one sense, they have the unfamiliarity of special items only brought out for special occasions. In day-to-day politics rights are often invoked—civil rights, gay rights, constitutional rights, even human rights, but very rarely or almost never unalienable rights. Political arguments are not advanced on the basis of self-evident truths; political debates feature the conflicting results of a torrent of policy studies and pronouncements by supposed experts instead.

Americans on all sides of the debate agree that something has gone wrong in American politics. Many Americans believe that we have lost our way because we no longer guide ourselves by the ideas of the Founders. But guiding ourselves by the Founders seems to be easier said than done. Could it be that part of our difficulty is that we no longer use, or even really understand, the language the Founders used or why they used that language? And if so, how did that come about?

This book is dedicated to the proposition that we need to understand the language of the Founders if we want to understand the ideas of the Founders.

It will also tell the story of the systematic effort to bury the ideas of the Founders.

Along the way we will consider "the Pursuit of Happiness" and "We the People" and other jewels of the American idea in the light of the Founders' original understanding.

As is so often the case, Lincoln said it best. Lincoln said the Founders gave us government by, for, and of the people. In America, government is in our hands.

Consequently, in the American idea of government, everything ultimately depends upon America's citizens. But citizens are made, not born. The gift of government by the people brings real responsibilities. Not the least of these is the citizen's responsibility to understand the American idea.

And in addition to understanding it, citizens in general must be dedicated to that idea if the nation is to thrive, or even to function at all well. That is the reason government officials from the President on down swear an oath to preserve, protect and defend the Constitution, America's charter of self-government.

And that is also the reason for the Founders' emphasis on the importance of education. Each of us must get the education necessary to become an American citizen. Here is Lincoln again: "The philosophy of the school room in one generation will be the philosophy of government in the next."

The bad news is that we were not taught the Founders' ideas or the language of the Founders when we were in the school room.

If we had been, then you and I would always have been ready to answer questions from a foreign visitor about Jefferson's immortal words in the Declaration with the greatest of ease.

That is why you want to read this book.

The good news is that understanding the language of the Founders and the ideas of the Founders is not difficult—and the rewards are great. Once you understand their thinking, all of the pieces will fit together. The Declaration of Independence and the Constitution will open themselves to your understanding.

The Founders intended it to be so. They meant for us to understand the American idea. That is one of the reasons the Declaration and the Constitution are so brief that a citizen can carry both of them printed together in a small, slim copy that slips easily into a shirt pocket. Armed with a good understanding of the American idea, the Declaration and the Constitution become our guidebooks for carrying out our responsibilities as American citizens.

This brief book is not intended for the scholar, but for the intelligent citizen who simply wants to understand the Founders.

In what follows, we will consider the Declaration's immortal statement of the principles of the Founders as well as other statements by the Founders in order to learn how they fit together, to discover the pattern of ideas that connects them. We will also examine some well-known comments about what the Founders meant from more recent times.

So this brief book does not focus on the obscure, but instead, for the most part, on the very familiar. In that sense, it only skims the surface, but it aims to do so in a way that reveals the depths.

If reading this little book quickens your interest to learn more, there is a wealth of fascinating material—and this book can get you oriented to make sense of whatever you choose to read.

If on the other hand, you simply want the maximum of understanding in the minimum of pages, then this is the book for you.

Introduction

As you know, the American Founders claimed they were guided by self-evident truths, truths "no sooner understood than they are believed" because they "carry the light of truth itself."

In order to understand the Declaration of Independence and the Constitution, we need to begin with the fact that the Founders' understanding of self-evident truth was based on the work of a Scottish philosopher named Thomas Reid. Reid was the founder of common sense realism, referred to by Prof. Arthur Herman on the page of quotes above.

Self-evident truths are the foundation of common sense realism, and they are a key to understanding the thinking of America's Founders.

America was truly blessed by the wisdom of the Founders. So remarkable are the Founders that many Americans believe Providence was at work in America's Founding. The evidence for that belief abounds. Washington was again and again miraculously protected from harm in battle. The illegitimate, orphaned Hamilton was whisked from obscurity on a remote Caribbean island to serve brilliantly at Washington's side in the war, at Yorktown and in the first administration as Treasury Secretary. These are just two examples in the marvelous chronicles of the gathering of the Founders. No wonder Washington believed Divine Providence had guided events.

The greatness of the Founding goes far beyond that awe-inspiring assembly of men. In designing the government and envisioning the nation, the Founders were quite consciously relying on and working with a well-considered set of arguments and ideas, arguments and ideas that were grounded in a new and profound understanding of human nature. The success of America's Founding was the result of the ideas that guided those men, as well as the greatness of the men who relied on those ideas.

Today in America, the greatness of the Founders has not been completely forgotten, but we have, for the most part, lost sight of the ideas that guided their deliberations. Many Americans believe what every schoolboy and every schoolgirl believes: the Founders took the ideas they used for the Founding from John Locke. Although it is widely believed, this version of the story of America stops short of the developments that made the Founding what it was. To understand the Founders' thinking, we must understand the American Enlightenment.

An American Enlightenment? The very idea may seem to you to be a surprising one. Wasn't the Enlightenment about the ideas of the French philosopher Voltaire and his followers? And aren't we told the Founders were basically down-to-earth, practical men of simple good sense? After all, the widely admired French commentator on America, Alexis de Tocqueville, famously wrote in 1831 that Americans were not interested in theoretical pursuits:

"I think that in no country in the civilized world is less attention
paid to philosophy than in the United States."

Books on America written in our day frequently quote these words
of Tocqueville as if they represent the authoritative final judgment
on American thought in the early period of the nation. But is it
true that the Founders merely took what ideas they needed from
Locke, and little more needs to be said about American thought
during the Founders' era?

As will become clear, there was an American Enlightenment,
and understanding it provides the key to unlocking many mysteries,
mysteries in the era of the American Founding, in American
Constitutional history up until the present and even in the direct
antecedents of the Founding reaching back to the sixteenth century.

In broad outline, the story is easy to follow.
John Locke established the foundation for political thought at
the beginning of the Enlightenment era. So great was Locke's
influence that in terms of politics the Enlightenment era could
be called the Age of Locke. Britain's Glorious Revolution of 1688
overthrew the last Stuart king and put an end to the Stuarts' claim
to unlimited royal sovereignty by divine right. Locke championed
the Glorious Revolution and the right of revolution. He also made
the case for limits on government power and for the consent of
the governed.

Despite the importance of Locke's political thinking, he had
a divided legacy. During the Enlightenment era, America and
France each had their own revolutions, but neither resembled
the British revolution of 1688. The French got political chaos, the
blood-drenched time of the Terror, and soon reverted to tyranny

again, this time under Napoleon. America got something new in the political history of humankind.

In the realm of political theory, France began by proceeding directly from Locke, or at least Voltaire believed he did. Voltaire was inspired by Locke ("never, perhaps, has a wiser, more methodical mind existed than Mr. Locke") and Sir Isaac Newton (a genius "the like of which has scarcely appeared in ten centuries"). From the example of Locke and Newton, Voltaire drew the conclusion that unassisted human reason could provide humanity with the answers to every question. He believed he was introducing English ways into France, starting with his *English Letters* in 1734 then setting to work on his *Elements of the Philosophy of Newton*. However, the Enlightenment of Voltaire and his French colleagues quickly took a radically different direction, perhaps a characteristically French one, certainly not an English one.

America's revolution too had a very different outcome than Britain's Glorious Revolution. The political thinking of the Founders had taken them beyond the ideas of the Glorious Revolution. The Americans were able to create political structure anew because they were thinking anew about mankind and the state.

That new thinking about mankind and the state is what the American Enlightenment is all about. The American Founding that resulted is still today the most radical attempt to establish a regime of liberty in the entire history of mankind.

The political genius of the Founders made the American Enlightenment one of the most remarkable developments in the history of the world. As Lord Acton wrote in his *Essays in the History of Liberty*, "Europe seemed incapable of becoming the home of free States. It was from America that the plain ideas . . . burst forth like a conqueror upon the world they were destined to transform, under the title of the Rights of Man."

Unlike the French, the Americans did not arrive at the American version of the Enlightenment by proceeding directly from Locke. Instead, the Americans got some help, and magnificent help it was. The American Enlightenment was informed by the Scottish Enlightenment. That is to say, the Americans benefitted from another of the most remarkable developments in the history of the world. The Scottish Enlightenment thinker Adam Smith gave us modern economics with his epoch-making book *The Wealth of Nations*. Smith's close friend James Hutton gave us modern geology and the modern concept of deep time. Smith and Hutton's close friend the chemist and physicist Joseph Black initiated the science of thermodynamics. Black helped another Scottish James, James Watt, also one of Smith's many friends, develop the steam engine. (Smith, a professor, helped Watt find workspace at Smith's university for his experiments.) The list goes on and on because the Scottish Enlightenment was, as it is said, "crowded with genius." The economics of Adam Smith and the discoveries of James Watt, Joseph Black and their colleagues powered the Industrial Revolution and opened the way to our modern world.

But it was mainly in philosophy that the Founders learned from the Scots. This was for the very good reason that the American Enlightenment was focused on the theory and practice of liberty. As we shall see, the Founders' understanding of "self-evident truths" and "unalienable rights" was rooted in the Scottish Enlightenment. The Scots gave the Founders a tremendous assist, and then America's Founders went far beyond their Scottish teachers in the realm of political thought.

Scottish Enlightenment philosophy was brought to these shores by a wave of enthusiastic scholars and clergy from Scotland, scholars like John Witherspoon and William Small who mentored Madison and Jefferson, and also by Americans like Benjamin Rush who went to Scotland to study.

The thinkers of the Scottish Enlightenment and the people who carried their ideas to America arrived just in time to provide the foundation for the American Enlightenment and to shape the American experiment. The Founders and the ideas they needed met in the historic moment.

Perhaps this matter of perfect timing is as remarkable as the men who received it and the remarkable use those men made of their opportunity.

Scottish Enlightenment philosophy was set in motion by Francis Hutcheson. Hutcheson taught philosophy at the University of Glasgow in Scotland from 1730 until his death in 1746. His concern was to make a philosophical case for the moral sense, but his impact was not restricted to this overriding concern. His profound analysis of rights gave us "unalienable rights", one of his greatest gifts to the Founders. Hutcheson mentored Adam Smith, the author of *The Moral Sentiments* and *The Wealth of Nations*, who in his turn held the same prestigious professorship. Thomas Reid succeeded Adam Smith in that same professorship.

Reid founded common sense realism, called by Arthur Herman "virtually the official creed of the American Republic" on the page of citations at the beginning of this book. Reid published his *An Inquiry into the Human Mind on the Principles of Common Sense* in 1764. In it he took a different lesson from Newton than did Voltaire. Voltaire drew the conclusion that unassisted human reason could answer all questions; for Reid, Newton taught "the way of observation and experiment":

> "Wise men now agree, or ought to agree, in this, that there is but one way to the knowledge of nature's works—the way of observation and experiment."

According to Reid, Newton's method was based on the capacity we all have to conduct our daily lives: "the first principles of all sciences are the dictates of common sense and lie open to all men."

As you know, the American Founders claimed they were guided by self-evident truths. For our purpose of understanding the Founders, the Declaration, and the Constitution, the important point is that their claims about self-evident truths reveal that their deliberations were deeply informed by the thinking of Thomas Reid. In addition, the prominence of the concept of unalienable rights shows that they had also carefully studied the works of Francis Hutcheson.

Despite what Tocqueville and others have written, there was a distinctively American philosophy at the Founding and during the life of the young American republic. Because that philosophy had deep roots in the Scottish Enlightenment the Scottish philosophical tradition was paramount in America's colleges. The distinguished American historian, Allen Guelzo, made that point in this way in his truly great lecture series, "The American Mind":

> "Before the Civil War, every major [American] collegiate intellectual was a disciple of Scottish common sense realism."

This accurate and important observation manages to say a great deal in a few words. It makes the important point.

For our purposes however, two brief additional comments may be helpful. Notice that by the time of the Civil War, this had been the American intellectual tradition for at least a century. Yet because of its deep roots in Scottish thought, the Scottish label endured, and is still used today when referring to the Americans who carried on the tradition long after the official end of the Scottish Enlightenment period in Scotland. This is remarkable testimony to the impact of the Scottish thinkers on American thought.

In addition, with the passage of time "common sense realism" came to do double duty. In its narrow use, it referred to Reid's philosophical work; used more broadly, as by Guelzo above, it became the shorthand term for the Scottish Enlightenment in general and also for the thought of Americans who continued to work in the moral sense and common sense tradition the Scots had founded. In part this broad use of the term reflects Reid's enormous prestige in America. Also, there was a need for a shorthand term; "moral sense philosophy and common sense realism" is simply too long to be handy. More fundamentally, Reid, following as he did Hutcheson and Adam Smith, in many ways encompassed their thinking. In addition, many believed then and believe now that Reid provided Scottish Enlightenment philosophy with its crowning achievement. All of these factors made common sense realism the natural choice for use as the shorthand label for the whole tradition.

If we want to understand the thinking of the Founders as revealed in the Declaration of Independence and the Constitution, we must first touch base with Thomas Reid and his Scottish colleagues. Is the importance of Reid and his colleagues to the

Founders news to you? Have you perhaps never even heard of Thomas Reid? If so, what that means is you have not been provided with the keys to understanding the thinking of the Founders.

The good news is that understanding their thinking is not going to be difficult for you. It is even fun, and it is well within your reach. All you need is common sense, and a brief survey of the territory so well known to the Founders, yet largely forgotten today.

As I will attempt to make clear, the ideas of Reid and his Scottish colleagues shaped the American Enlightenment, the American experiment and American political thought.

There is one point I must emphasize: to say the Scottish Enlightenment shaped the American experiment is not to diminish in any way the achievements of the Founders. Their astonishing achievements are in the first rank in the whole history of the world. To get a clear view of the tallest mountain peak, you may need to be standing on a nearby peak—and to be facing in the right direction. To understand the Founders, we need to understand on whose shoulders the Founders were standing.

This book was written as a series of individual studies over a period of years. These studies have an overarching unity of purpose. They are the record of the explorations and discoveries I made as I pursued a path of understanding. That path kept revealing itself to me as I progressed. I could not have said ahead of time what I was going to learn along the way. Each study I have included here selects a strategic point over the buried past. These strategic points reveal the hidden outline of what has been lost.

As a result of my journey, I can report to you that understanding the thinking of the Founders is a task worth doing. It is also the citizen's duty and the patriot's joyful obligation.

Introduction

I begin with the conventional wisdom regarding Locke and the Glorious Revolution.

OVERTURE

Locke's Revolution

"The supreme power in every commonwealth [is] but the joint power of every member of the society."
—JOHN LOCKE, *TWO TREATISES OF GOVERNMENT*

No doubt this statement strikes you as merely a truism.

That it does is testimony to the influence of John Locke. It is very difficult for us today to comprehend how radical this claim was at the time it was made, and how dangerous it was for Locke to make it. In England, and elsewhere, the royal sovereign was the supreme power. For Locke to have simply linked his name to the statement, as I have done at the top of the page, would have meant his death.

In 1683, taking the unpublished manuscript of the *Treatises* with him, Locke managed to get himself smuggled out of England to safety in Holland. Agents of Charles II, who claimed absolute sovereignty by divine right, were in hot pursuit of him. The manuscript when eventually published contained this passage:

"Absolute monarchy is inconsistent with Civil Society, and so can be no form of Civil Government at all."

Having such thoughts then could be fatal. If Locke had been caught, the king would not have needed the damning evidence of that manuscript. Locke had already become too closely associated with opposition to Charles' rule to be safe in England.

Locke only returned to Britain when he escorted the princess of Orange from Holland to become Queen Mary. The Glorious Revolution of 1688 had put an end to the Stuart kings' claim to absolute sovereignty by divine right, and established a monarchy of limited powers under William and Mary.

The *Two Treatises of Government* did not appear until 1690, and even then they were published anonymously. Locke only acknowledged his authorship in a codicil to his will. Although it had been written before the revolution, the preface claimed that the work was intended to justify Britain's Glorious Revolution, "to establish the Throne of Our Great Restorer, our present King William; to make good his Title, in the Consent of the People."

What was politically possible for revolution to achieve in Britain in 1688 was a monarchy of somewhat limited powers, limited at least by a Bill of Rights which guaranteed the people some basic protections from governmental power. When nearly a century later the Founders staked their lives, their fortunes and their sacred honor on the American bid for liberty, it was to Locke that the Founders turned to justify their right to revolution and to government by the consent of the people. However, very different circumstances made it possible for the Founders to go much further than what was accomplished by the Glorious Revolution. No doubt the Founders went even further than Locke imagined, but Locke had staked out the basis of their claim to liberty.

When independence was won, the American Founders did not follow the example of the Glorious Revolution by setting up a parliament and a monarchy in America. Much had happened in America by 1776 that explains the very different form of government that came out of the American Revolution.

A look into the colonial college named in honor of William and Mary can give us a clue about that different outcome. As a student at William and Mary, Thomas Jefferson came under the influence of William Small. Small, who mentored Jefferson during his time at college and afterwards, was a member in good standing of the Scottish Enlightenment. He came to America from Scotland to teach at William and Mary just in time to guide Jefferson's studies there during the most intellectually influential years of Jefferson's life.

In the same way, John Witherspoon, another full-fledged member of the Scottish Enlightenment, mentored James Madison at Princeton. In addition, the tutors who educated Jefferson and Madison before college were also Scots. All these Scots were part of a wave of scholars and clergy that brought the ideas of the Scottish Enlightenment to colonial America.

The Founders did not make George Washington a monarch, nor did they design a parliament on the British model. They did not provide for an aristocracy; in fact they ruled out an aristocracy. They also ruled out a politically empowered church allied with the government. The Founders made a radical break with the past. They set out to do what had not been done before: to design a system whereby the people of a geographically extended and diverse territory would govern themselves. They boldly went where none had gone before.

The Scots had provided the Founders with radically new ideas that were to enable them to fashion government along unprecedented lines—and to find a hitherto undreamed of way to realize Locke's revolutionary claim that the supreme political power in every commonwealth is the people. When it came time to lay the foundation for the new nation and its government, the Founders went to work thoroughly grounded in the philosophical arguments the Scots advanced. It was those arguments that showed the Founders a way forward. It enabled them to go beyond the idea of a monarchy with its power somewhat limited by a Bill of Rights, and to make the American experiment in government by, for, and of the people.

ONE

The Founders

"It is rare indeed for a nation to have at its summit a group so variously gifted as Washington and Benjamin Franklin, Thomas Jefferson, Alexander Hamilton, James Madison, and John Adams. And what was particularly providential was the way in which their strengths and weaknesses compensated each other, so that the group as a whole was infinitely more formidable than the sum of its parts. They were the Enlightenment made flesh."

—PAUL JOHNSON, *A HISTORY OF THE AMERICAN PEOPLE*

EDUCATING THE FOUNDERS

"At age sixteen Jefferson and Madison and Hamilton were all being schooled by Scots who had come to America as adults."
—GARRY WILLS, *INVENTING AMERICA*

This remarkable fact was no mere coincidence. Scholars from Scotland were held in the highest regard in colonial America because of the preeminence of Scottish thinkers and Scottish universities at that time. The Scottish Enlightenment (it is usually dated from about 1730 until the 1790's) was an explosion of creative intellectual energy in science, philosophy, economics, and technological innovation. It arrived just in time to have a decisive influence on the Founders.

Jefferson was the architect of the Declaration of Independence, Madison was the architect of the Constitution, and Hamilton was the architect of *The Federalist Papers*. If we want to understand their thinking, we need to start with the fact that the Scottish Enlightenment provided their teachers.

Jefferson's tutor, William Douglas, had studied at Glasgow and Edinburgh, but the great intellectual influence on Jefferson was William Small. Small was a powerful representative of the Scottish Enlightenment, and he was by far the most brilliant member of the faculty at William and Mary. He came to America to teach only from 1758 to 1764—at precisely the right time to guide Jefferson's studies there. Small left America when he did in response to an urgent request from James Watt. Watt wanted his help with the development of the steam engine.

Madison's tutor, Donald Robertson, was also a product of the Scottish Enlightenment at its peak, but the great intellectual influence on Madison was John Witherspoon, also a Scot. Witherspoon's own education can help us see just how close the Founders were to the Scottish Enlightenment. Before coming to America, he studied with Adam Smith and Thomas Reid. When Madison entered Princeton in 1769, under the leadership of Witherspoon it had become the American university where the great thinkers of the Scottish Enlightenment—Francis Hutcheson, Thomas Reid, Adam Smith, Adam Ferguson and David Hume—were studied most intensely.

Hamilton set out from the island of St. Croix to enroll at Princeton in 1772. He was sent by two sponsors who had recognized his astonishing gifts, his employer and Hugh Knox, a Scot and a Presbyterian minister who was a Princeton graduate. Upon his arrival, Hamilton met with Witherspoon and proposed that he be allowed to blaze through his studies at a rate only determined by his intellectual powers. When Witherspoon turned down his bold proposal, Hamilton made the same proposal at King's College (today's Columbia) and was accepted. His tutor there, Robert Harpur, was also a product of the Scottish Enlightenment, having studied at Glasgow before coming to America.

The ideas of the Scottish Enlightenment were studied and hotly debated just about everywhere in colonial America. In the words of the eminent scholar Douglass Adair, "At Princeton, at William and Mary, at Pennsylvania, at Yale, at King's, and at Harvard, the young men who rode off to war in 1776 had been trained in the texts of Scottish social science." James Foster's admirable book *Scottish Philosophy in America* states it this way:

"The Scottish Enlightenment provided the fledgling United States of America and its emerging universities with a philosophical orientation. For a hundred years or more, Scottish philosophers were both taught and emulated by professors at Princeton, Harvard and Yale, as well as newly founded colleges stretching from Rhode Island to Texas."

Foster's thoughtful and useful work provides brief discussions of the major figures from Witherspoon, Benjamin Rush, and James Wilson in the Founders' generation to James McCosh late in the nineteenth century. McCosh, the president of Princeton for twenty years beginning in 1868, continued to work in the tradition of common sense realism throughout his long career. He published prolifically, wrote in a clear and readable style, and exerted a significant intellectual influence on American thought.

It is well known that the Founders were on the whole remarkable for their learning. It is fair to say that by modern standards they were as a group almost unimaginably learned. They knew their Aristotle, they knew their Cicero, and they knew the Bible—and often read the texts in the original languages; Jefferson and Adams read Greek, Latin and Hebrew. They knew their Shakespeare, and they knew their Locke.

What is not so well known is how much the Scots contributed to the Founders' thinking. In this book we will examine some of the best known writings of the Founders. And everywhere we look, we will encounter the imprint of the Scots. If you study the American Enlightenment it is difficult to avoid recognizing the contribution of the Scots. Those who overlook the Scots' contributions to the American Founding end up overlooking the American Enlightenment itself.

Witherspoon is no doubt the most important example of the influence of Scottish educators. In the words of Jeffry Morrison in his biography of Witherspoon:

> "No other founder (not even James Wilson) did more to channel the Scottish philosophy into the colonies and thus into American political thought."

Witherspoon's students by one count included, among many others, five delegates to the Constitutional Convention, twenty-eight U.S. senators, forty-nine U.S. representatives, twelve governors, three Supreme Court Justices, eight U.S. district judges, three attorneys general, and many members of state constitutional conventions and state ratifying conventions. Is it any wonder that the ideas and arguments of Reid and Smith and their Scottish colleagues are everywhere in the writings of the Founders?

Witherspoon's course in moral philosophy, which he dictated year after year in largely unchanging form and which his students copied down faithfully, is almost certainly the most influential single college course in America's history. It borrowed heavily from Hutcheson's *A System of Moral Philosophy*, and at its core were the principles of Reid's common sense realism:

> "[There are] certain principles or dictates of common sense . . . These are the foundation of all reasoning . . . They can no more be proved than an axiom in mathematical science."

Henry May, in his book *The Enlightenment in America*, points to Witherspoon's lectures as the source of "the long American career of Scottish Common Sense" which was "to rule American college teaching for almost a century."

Princeton was founded by the Presbyterians to provide a college in America for the training of its ministers for America. The American Presbyterian Church was a powerful and united religious organization in the Founders' generation, and this was an era in which the pulpit mattered to an extent that is very nearly inconceivable to Americans today. As the de facto head of the Presbyterians in America, Witherspoon's influence was enormous, reaching American communities far removed from college campuses.

Beyond his enormous influence as an educator and church leader, Witherspoon was also one of the most important of the Founders. He was an early and influential champion of American independence, and much more than merely a signer of the Declaration of Independence. In fact, he played a central role in the signing.

When the Declaration was completed and ready to be signed, the signers-to-be wavered. For two days they hesitated to affix their signatures. To sign it, after all, was to provide the British with documentary evidence of treason, punishable by death. Witherspoon rose to the occasion, speaking in his famously thick Scottish accent:

> "There is a tide in the affairs of men, a nick of time. We perceive it now before us. To hesitate is to content to our own slavery. That noble instrument upon your table, which ensures immortality to its author, should be subscribed this very morning by every pen in this house. He that will not respond to its accents

and strain every nerve to carry into effect its provisions is unworthy the name freeman."

His speech broke the logjam and, as we all know, the delegates then swiftly signed the Declaration.

BENJAMIN RUSH'S STORY

"The Revolution was effected before the war commenced. The Revolution was in the minds and hearts of the people . . . This radical change in the principles, opinions, sentiments, and affections of the people, was the real American Revolution."
—JOHN ADAMS

The people of the thirteen colonies had to break free of the idea that they were subjects in order to become citizens. As Gordon Wood writes in *The American Revolution*:

"Since the king, in the words of the English jurist William Blackstone, was the 'pater familias of the nation,' to be a subject was in fact to be a kind of child . . . [The people] had to be held together from above, by the power of kings who created trains of dependencies and inequalities, supported by standing armies, strong religious establishments, and a dazzling array of titles, rituals, and ceremonies."

To declare, as the Founders did, that the people are sovereign was to think and feel in a new way. After all, at that time "the sovereign" was the chief of state, that is, the king or the queen.

Benjamin Rush provides a fascinating example of how that change in feeling and thinking occurred, and at the same time his story tells us something very important about the American Founding.

A signer of the Declaration of Independence and surgeon general in Washington's army, Rush was an early and influential agitator for American independence who wrote of "the absurdity of hereditary power." Yet when he had set out for Scotland to study medicine, he was a thoroughgoing monarchist: "I had been taught to consider [kings] nearly as essential to political order as the Sun is to the order of our Solar System." By the time he returned home to Philadelphia in 1769 he was a revolutionary committed to republican government.

After graduating from Princeton, Rush traveled to Scotland to study medicine at Edinburgh. In the colonial era, Scottish universities were generally recognized as the world's best, and Edinburgh was considered the world's foremost medical school. Rush studied there under William Cullen, then the medical school's star attraction. Cullen was one of the luminaries of the Scottish Enlightenment, and the other luminaries of the Scottish Enlightenment were his patients and friends. A cousin of Thomas Reid became one of Rush's closest friends. Rush had, quite characteristically for him, landed in the center of the action.

Rush had an uncanny knack for being in the right place at the right time. It is difficult to overestimate the importance of John Witherspoon's role in the Founding—and Rush, while studying in Scotland, played a key role in persuading Witherspoon to accept the invitation to become the president of Princeton and also in overcoming Mrs. Witherspoon's resolute opposition to moving to America.

It is equally difficult to overestimate the importance of Tom Paine's *Common Sense*. *Common Sense* was read by virtually every American who could read, and read aloud to those who could not. It had a decisive influence on American public sentiment in favor of the Revolution. In it Paine elevated the idea of common sense thinking in America while at the same time subjecting monarchy and especially hereditary monarchy to a devastating critique:

> "One of the strongest natural proofs of the folly of hereditary right in Kings, is that nature disproves it, otherwise she would not so frequently turn it into ridicule, by giving mankind an *Ass for a Lion.*" [Italics in original]

After Rush returned to America, he urged Paine to write *Common Sense*, supplied Paine with many of the ideas and even convinced Paine to use that title.

Rush seemed always to be where the action was, even when it came to the effort of getting the Constitution approved. At first, the prospects for approval looked dim. As the struggle played out, the battle in Pennsylvania became critical. Pennsylvania's eventual vote for approval helped to turn the tide. How did that vote come about? Much credit goes to Rush. With James Wilson playing the lead, together they conducted the very effective campaign that made the difference in Pennsylvania.

Rush was what today we would call a networker. He knew everybody, and everybody knew him. What is remarkable about his network is the story it tells about the Founding. Rush's network of contacts is a who's who of the Scottish Enlightenment and of the American Founding. Before leaving this page, ponder for just a moment the fact that Rush's network included Adam Smith and David Hume, Benjamin Franklin and George Washington.

***

THE CONSTITUTIONAL CONVENTION AS DRAMA
"After Madison, [James] Wilson's was the most important hand in shaping the Constitution . . ."
—Paul Johnson, *A History of the American People*

Remarkably, the actual course of events during the Constitutional Convention, as if by dramatic intent, seems designed to draw our attention to the enormous importance of the Scottish Enlightenment in America's Founding.

If we consider the Constitutional Convention as a dramatic work, James Madison and James Wilson got the roles that drove the action. Madison opened with the Virginia Plan; Wilson played a central role in the debate and in the final decisive action, the drafting of the Constitution by the committee that gave it the shape we know today.

Their central roles dramatize the impact of the Scottish Enlightenment because Madison and Wilson taken together perfectly symbolize that impact.

Madison symbolizes one half of the story of the Scots in America. He represents the Revolutionary generation of Americans trained by the wave of Scots who brought the Scottish Enlightenment to America. As we have seen, Madison's tutor, Donald Robertson, was a product of the Scottish Enlightenment at its peak, and Madison's mentor was the Scottish educator John Witherspoon.

Madison was steeped in the Scottish tradition. His education was so strongly Scottish in its character that until the end of his life he spoke French with a marked Scottish accent.

As for Wilson, he is a perfect symbol for the other half of the story. He was actually a part of that wave of Scots in America. A member in good standing of the Scottish Enlightenment, he was educated at St. Andrews, Glasgow and Edinburgh at the height of the Scottish Enlightenment. On stage, in our Constitutional-Convention-as-drama, we would be constantly reminded of the Scottish influence by Wilson's strong Scottish accent.

It is important to remember that Wilson was not a second-tier figure. Wilson is only slightly outside the small circle of the Founders we all know. His contemporaries would be surprised to learn that he is not better remembered today. He was a member of that most select group of the Founders; he was one of only six men who signed both the Declaration and the Constitution. Washington appointed him to the very first Supreme Court, making him a member of yet another very select group among the Founders. So great was Wilson's standing at the time that many Americans expected, and it was rumored in the press, that Washington would select him to be America's first Chief Justice. In the event, Washington selected John Jay instead and that is perhaps the reason Wilson's name eventually fell from the list of the Founders everyone knows.

For our Constitutional-Convention-as-drama, the main point is that these two characters who symbolize the story of the Scottish Enlightenment in America drive the action. In addition, our production includes two dramatic devices that brilliantly highlight the significance of Madison and Wilson.

First, they are elevated by being closely associated with the two most esteemed men in the room—George Washington and Benjamin Franklin. Everyone in the room knew that Madison spoke for Washington; he was even seated to Washington's right and beside the dais from which Washington presided. In much the same way, Wilson was paired with Franklin. This was also clear to everyone in the room. Wilson read Franklin's prepared statements for him. To appreciate the dramatic power of these pairings, we only need to keep in mind just how much Washington and Franklin were the very symbols of America. Washington, "the Father of the Country," and Franklin, "the First American," were for Americans of that time their country's two iconic figures.

In addition, the dramatic impact of Madison and Wilson's pairing with Washington and Franklin is greatly enhanced by the comparative silence of the two icons. Washington rarely spoke, confining himself to the role of president of the Convention. Except for the prepared statements Wilson read for him, Franklin also limited his remarks to a few critical moments when his enormous prestige was needed to make a way forward. Their brilliant junior associates conducted the campaign. Madison and Wilson, our symbols of the Scottish Enlightenment's impact on America, are given center stage.

Considered purely as drama, pairing Wilson the Scot and Madison the Scottish-educated American with the two great icons of America, and giving Wilson and Madison their key roles in the debate seems designed, as if by Providence, to send us today a potent reminder of the importance of the Scottish Enlightenment to the American Enlightenment and, therefore, to America's Founding.

THE FOUNDERS' TRADITION

"We have had to the present day two different traditions in the theory of liberty . . . [one] was made explicit mainly by a group of Scottish moral philosophers . . . Opposed to them was the tradition of the French Enlightenment."
—F. A. HAYEK, *THE CONSTITUTION OF LIBERTY*

Hayek's point is important because it highlights the decisive influence of the Scottish Enlightenment on the Founders' thinking on liberty. The Founders were steeped in the Scottish tradition. As Daniel Walker Howe put it, "the Scots spread a rich intellectual table from which the Americans could pick and choose and feast."

The Scottish Enlightenment was made up of men who delighted in vigorous debate. And yet, as Samuel Fleischacker has written in his outstanding essay "Scottish Philosophy and the American Founding":

"The Scots did tend to share some general views—on the sociability of human nature, on the importance of history to moral philosophy and social science, on the dignity and intelligence of ordinary people—that were of great importance to their followers in America and elsewhere."

Those shared general views informed the American debate, and provided the basis of a fundamental agreement among the Founders.

This fundamental agreement is a matter of the utmost importance. In the words of Thomas West in his brilliant essay "The Universal Principles of the American Founding":

"One of the striking things about the leading men [of the American Founding] is how different they were in their particular preoccupations, and yet how much they agreed on principles."

How different our history might have been if there had been a significant party among the Founders committed to the ideas of the French Enlightenment. It was our great good fortune that there was not.

THE FOUNDING

"The Americans are the first people whom Heaven has favored with an opportunity of deliberating upon, and choosing, the forms of government under which they shall live."

—JOHN JAY

The great political writings of the American Enlightenment— the Declaration of Independence, the Constitution, and *The Federalist Papers*—are quite properly included in collections of Enlightenment writings. They are among the greatest works of the Enlightenment era. Yet even Americans who are interested in American history usually do not see them as having anything to do with the Enlightenment.

How did this happen?

Although the Enlightenment began in England, with the passage of time the French Enlightenment gained prominence, eventually eclipsing all of the other developments in the Enlightenment era. More and more, the French Enlightenment came to be identified with the Enlightenment itself. As a result, gener-

28

alizations about the Enlightenment today all too often end up actually being generalizations about the French Enlightenment.

It is easy to find examples of even those who should know better falling victim to this tendency. *The Portable Enlightenment Reader* is an excellent collection of writings of the Enlightenment era. In his introduction to the book, the editor, Isaac Kramnick, writes: "The Enlightenment was an international movement that included French, English, Scottish, American, German, Italian, Spanish, and even Russian schools." On the very next page he also writes: "What was the message of these Enlightenment intellectuals? . . . They believed that unassisted human reason, not faith or tradition, was the principle guide to human conduct." This is a perfectly fair characterization of the French Enlightenment, which the noted scholar Gertrude Himmelfarb aptly calls "the ideology of reason." However, as for the Scottish and the American Enlightenments, it completely misses the mark.

The Founders did not believe that unassisted human reason was the principle guide to human conduct, nor did the Scots. For the Founders and for the Scots, human reason is able to function as a guide to human conduct only when grounded in the moral sense. For example, here is Thomas Jefferson on this subject:

> "State a moral case to a ploughman and a professor. The former will decide it as well and often better than the latter, because he has not been led astray by artificial rules."

In precisely the same way, they believed reason can provide knowledge and human understanding only when reason is grounded in common sense.

Because they did not assign primacy to unassisted human reason, the Founders do not fit the prevailing image of Enlightenment thinkers. The Founders were not like the French *philosophes*, and the *philosophes* are now the very models of the Enlightenment.

Yet it seems to me that there is another reason why Americans today tend not to recognize *The Federalist Papers*, for example, as a classic of the Enlightenment. It is not for us a curious antique document that is marooned in that era in the remote past. The French remember the French Enlightenment, but no one today reads the *Encyclopédie*, the work that symbolized the French Enlightenment. The *philosophes* of the Enlightenment era have been displaced many times over by new fashions in French thought—romanticism, socialism, existentialism, postmodernism—but *The Federalist Papers* continues to play a living part in the political and intellectual life of our republic today.

It is also true that the Founders did not labor to draw out for us the connections and the differences between their thinking and the thinking of others of the Enlightenment era. Had they very carefully done so for us there would be little need for this book, but they had more urgent and important tasks.

Jay was one of the authors of *The Federalist Papers* and the first Chief Justice of the United States. He, like the other Founders, was not concerned to trace for us the philosophical background of the Founding. The Founders were in the act of creation. They were focused on the great task before them, the urgent challenge and enormous opportunity of founding a republic that would not fail, as Athenian democracy and the Roman Republic had, but would survive to reach our own time and beyond.

Consequently, the Founding can be thought of as a kind of historical Big Bang, the brilliance of which eclipses its antecedents, obscuring even the American Enlightenment itself. Not guessing that we would eventually lose sight of the American Enlightenment, and therefore of the debt the American Enlightenment owed to the thinkers of Scottish Enlightenment, the Founders cannot be faulted for keeping their focus instead on making clear to us what they had given us: as Franklin famously said, " A republic, if you can keep it."

TWO

The American Enlightenment

". . . America was the embodiment and natural home of the Enlightenment . . ."
—ISAAC KRAMNICK, *THE ENLIGHTENMENT READER*

UNDERSTANDING JEFFERSON

"Man was destined for society . . . He was endowed with a sense
of right and wrong merely relative to this. This sense is as much
a part of his nature as the sense of hearing, seeing, feeling; it is
the true foundation of morality . . . The moral sense, or con-
science, is as much a part of a man as his leg or arm. It is given to
all human beings in a stronger or weaker degree . . . It may be
strengthened by exercise, as may any particular limb of the body.
This sense is submitted indeed in some degree to the guidance of
reason; but it is a small stock [amount] which is required for this."

—THOMAS JEFFERSON

This passage is taken from a letter to his nephew written in 1787, and repeated almost verbatim in a letter to John Adams twenty-eight years later. Here, in the language of Francis Hutcheson, the founder of Scottish moral sense philosophy, Jefferson presents the theory of human nature according to the Scottish and the American Enlightenments: man the social being, endowed with a moral sense and unalienable rights.

The emphasis on the moral sense, and also common sense, sharply distinguish both the Scottish Enlightenment and the American Enlightenment from the Enlightenment in France. As the Jefferson passage illustrates, the thinkers of the Scottish Enlightenment gave the Founders many of the ideas and the arguments they needed for the great task of the Founding.

The American Enlightenment was driven forward by a focus on the theory and practice of political liberty. With the exception of the scientific and technological achievements of Benjamin Franklin, the great works of the American Enlightenment are the Declaration of Independence, the Constitution, and *The Federalist Papers*. In articulating the principles and fashioning the institutions that would sustain the new republic, Jefferson and the other Founders made for themselves a place of honor among the greatest thinkers of the Enlightenment era.

TWO VISIONS OF THE ENLIGHTENMENT

"Fontenelle [was] the most representative of all the figures of the Enlightenment . . ."

—Isaiah Berlin

"If America was the embodiment and natural home of the Enlightenment . . . then the American who best personified the Enlightenment ideal was Benjamin Franklin."

—Isaac Kramnick

My copy of Professor Kramnick's book *The Portable Enlightenment Reader* has Benjamin West's famous painting *Benjamin Franklin Drawing Electricity from the Sky* on its cover. If Professor Berlin had selected the cover illustration, perhaps he would have chosen a portrait of Fontenelle instead.

Bernard Le Bovier de Fontenelle was a member of the French Academy and of the French Academy of Sciences. Berlin explains that he led a "very careful and rational life." Fontenelle, he also tells us, wrote this: "A work of politics, of morality, of criticism, perhaps even of literature, will be finer, all things considered, if made by the hands of a geometer." A geometer is, of course, a person skilled in geometry, that is to say, a person skilled in abstract, mathematical reasoning.

35

These two eminent scholars present two very different visions of the Enlightenment. According to one vision, the Enlightenment's center of gravity was unquestionably in France and its ideal was skillfulness in abstract rationality. Fontenelle displays very clearly the French Enlightenment's exaltation of "unassisted reason," of abstract rationality. Note that he claims that skill in abstract reasoning of the mathematical kind provides the best thinking about morality and politics. He goes beyond this remarkable claim even to claim that someone who is good at geometry might well have exactly what is needed to produce the best in literature. If this claim strikes you as unlikely, you have for yourself a measure of just how distant your own thinking is from the thinking of the French Enlightenment.

Franklin personified a very different vision of the Enlightenment. Capturing the incredible range of Franklin's gifts and the extent of his contributions is a challenge—and "abstract rationality" doesn't even come close.

Taking our cue from Benjamin West's painting, the story of Franklin's lightning experiment is a great place to begin. Franklin did more than just explain lightning, more even than lay the foundation for our modern understanding of electricity. He went on to make an urgently-needed practical application of his new-found scientific understanding by developing the world-changing technology of the lightning rod. Then he published the technological know-how, sharing it freely with the world. He demonstrated that we could understand nature and that our understanding of nature could change the world for the better for everyone. If a church happened to be struck by lightning and burned to the ground, it meant that the church fathers had neglected to install a lightning rod, not that last Sunday's sermon had found disfavor with God.

Here Franklin the scientist and technological innovator meets up with Franklin the philanthropist who instigated, organized and supported financially and otherwise so many projects to improve the lives of his fellow Philadelphians.

Of course, Franklin the statesman played an important role in shaping both the Declaration and the Constitution, two of the most world-changing achievements of the American Enlightenment, and of the Enlightenment overall. Characteristically, in the course of his many trips back and forth across the Atlantic in the political service of the colonies and the new nation, he also seized the opportunity to discover and map (modern satellites confirm quite accurately) the Gulf Stream, improving trans-Atlantic travel by ship forever. Franklin, the man who has been called "the First American," genuinely seemed to welcome every opportunity in his life-long adventure of making a better world.

For Thomas Reid, as we have noted, Newton's rules for doing science were "the way of observation and experiment." Franklin the scientist is a perfect exemplar of Newton's method. But there was more to Franklin than Newton's method, and more to the American Enlightenment than even Franklin can symbolize.

In any case, by now it should be clear that there is a world of difference between the French Enlightenment and the American Enlightenment. Consequently, when someone makes a general statement about the Enlightenment, we need to ask "which Enlightenment?"

SORTING OUT THE ENLIGHTENMENTS

If we set out to get clear about the various Enlightenments, Gertrude Himmelfarb's *The Roads to Modernity: The British, French, and American Enlightenments* ought to provide us with the answers we are looking for—and, in many ways, it does. Where the book is good, it is very good indeed. Unfortunately, although the author accomplishes the task brilliantly in two magnificent chapters, she also creates confusion in a third chapter.

The two outstanding chapters are the ones on the French and the American Enlightenments. They are models of brevity, clarity, and scholarly command of the subject. The French and the American Enlightenments are brought into sharp focus, and their profound differences are made clear.

Professor Himmelfarb brilliantly contrasts the French Enlightenment, which she terms "the Ideology of Reason," and the American Enlightenment, termed by her as "the Politics of Liberty":

"The idea of liberty . . . did not elicit anything like the passion or commitment [from the French] that reason did. Nor did it inspire the philosophes to engage in a systematic analysis of the political and social institutions that would promote and protect liberty."

The French *philosophes* and the American Founders were working in very different directions on very different projects. These differences help explain the sharply contrasting outcomes of the American and the French Revolutions.

Because the study of the Enlightenment has traditionally focused on France, these two chapters provide the interested reader with an opportunity to make a great leap forward not just in understanding the Enlightenments, but also in understanding America. Himmelfarb's thoughtful analysis makes a powerful case for the significance and the uniqueness of the American Enlightenment.

Himmelfarb also ably demonstrates that the *philosophes'* concept of reason explains their disdain for the common people. Voltaire, for example, never concealed that disdain, habitually referring to the people as *"la canaille"* (the rabble), and Diderot wrote that "the common people are incredibly stupid." The *philosophes'* statements about mankind are very different from Jefferson's comparison of a ploughman and a professor quoted above or his ringing declaration that "all men are created equal . . . endowed by their Creator with certain unalienable Rights . . ."

What explains this difference? Himmelfarb correctly assigns the difference to the role of two conceptions that were elevated to great prominence during the Enlightenment, the moral sense and common sense. Moral sense and common sense doctrines were central to the American Enlightenment:

"The moral sense and common sense . . . gave to all people, including the common people, a common humanity and a common fund of moral and social obligations. The French idea of reason was not available to the common people and had no such moral or social component."

Much ink has been spilled on the question of why the French and the American Revolutions had such different outcomes. Here you have a key difference, stated with brilliant clarity. The difference between the *philosophes* and the Founders is this: the primacy of unassisted reason versus the primacy of the moral sense and common sense.

However, always pairing the moral sense and common sense, as Himmelfarb very correctly does, raises a problem. The moral sense and common sense together practically define Scottish Enlightenment philosophy. This is so well established that the heading for a chapter on the Scottish Enlightenment virtually writes itself: "The Moral Sense and Common Sense." Yet there is no chapter on the Scottish Enlightenment. Instead, there is a single chapter combining the English and the Scottish Enlightenments under the single label of the British Enlightenment. Combining these two very different Enlightenments obscures an important part of the story.

The Enlightenment certainly began in England. It began with the publication of Newton's *Principia* in 1687, the Glorious Revolution of 1688, and the publication of the first of Locke's *Letters on Toleration* in 1689. But the Scots soon achieved prominence in the Enlightenment project, especially in science and in philosophy.

In philosophy, Locke's theory of the mind quickly got the Scots' attention. As you may remember from school, according to Locke the mind is like a sheet of blank paper. Experience writes on that blank sheet by means of sensations of pain and pleasure.

It is important for us to understand that Locke was not himself a skeptic; he believed that there are things that people know and he believed that there really is right and wrong. However, David Hume and others showed that Locke's account of the mind left the door wide open for skeptical challenges. So Francis Hutcheson, Adam Smith, and Thomas Reid set out to provide what was missing.

Francis Hutcheson set himself the task of finding a philosophical foundation for moral judgments. In doing so, he put Scottish Enlightenment philosophy in motion, and at the same time, put moral philosophy at the center of Scottish thought. He argued for the existence of the moral sense, relying on the analogy of our external senses, just as Jefferson, himself relying on Hutcheson, did in the earlier quote:

> "Man was destined for society . . . He was endowed with a sense of right and wrong merely relative to this. This sense is as much a part of his nature as the sense of hearing, seeing, feeling; it is the true foundation of morality."

Hutcheson believed that Locke's account, based as it was only on pleasure and pain, left convention as the only possible foundation of morality.

As modern persons, you and I have had moral relativism, the view of morality as convention, hammered into our heads in the classroom and by popular culture. As a result, we are perfectly familiar with its catechism: moral claims only reflect the conditioning by society about what we are to approve of or condemn, and so on. But, in defense of the Scots and the Founders, this is not how we understand moral claims when we actually make them. Despite efforts to convince you that those who commit *jihad* simply have a different definition of what is morally good than you do, if the victim of *jihad* is your daughter, your mother, your brother, you are likely to be certain that a real and terrible wrong has been committed.

Human beings simply are moral agents. We hold ourselves and others to moral standards, and we begin making moral claims almost as soon as we can talk. C. S. Lewis in *Mere Christianity* makes the point this way:

"Everyone has heard people quarreling . . . They say things like this: 'How'd you like it if anyone did the same to you?' . . . 'Leave him alone, he isn't doing you any harm' . . . Now what interests me about all these remarks is that the man who makes them is not merely saying that the other man's behavior does not happen to please him . . . they might, of course, fight like animals, but . . . [that would not be quarreling] in the human sense of the word. Quarrelling means trying to show that the other man is in the wrong."

The Nobel prize-winning Russian author Aleksandr Solzhenitsyn said it like this: "We are born with a sense of justice in our souls; we can't and don't want to live without it!"

Hutcheson in his time dedicated himself to the task of making the philosophical case for a moral sense. According to Hutcheson, our moral sense is an endowment of our human nature. A person's moral sense, like the sense of sight or hearing, is part of a person's human nature, part of what makes us the kind of creature we are.

Hutcheson's student Adam Smith developed his vision of man the moral and social being in two great works. *The Theory of Moral Sentiments* grounded morality in mankind's moral and social nature. In *The Wealth of Nations*, the foundation of modern economics, Smith demonstrated that economic activity is also grounded in mankind's moral and social nature.

Thomas Reid, next in line, expanded Hutcheson's vision of the specifically human endowment. Reid's philosophical purpose was a unifying explanation of the "phenomena of human nature" in terms of "the original powers and laws of our constitution." He was concerned to provide a philosophical foundation for morality and for knowledge. He argued that there is an endowment of human nature that makes possible both moral knowledge and human knowledge in general. Reid called it common sense. Because we possess it, we human beings can master speech, geometry, ship building, and a host of skills that are unique to humankind. It enables us to serve on a jury and weigh the evidence presented in a trial. By means of it we are able to make rational judgments, our defining power as reflected in the name given to our species, *Homo sapiens*.

Animals fulfill Locke's criteria in so far as they experience the impact of sensations of pain and pleasure, but they do not acquire thereby the ability to discover, learn and teach the Pythagorean Theorem, just as they do not thereby become moral agents. Giovanni B. Grandi put it like this in his introduction to Reid's collected writings:

> "According to Reid, there is an unbridgeable gap between animals and human beings . . . humans have the power . . . to act on the basis of rational judgments they can form about what is useful in the long-run and morally right."

Reidian common sense is that human attribute which sets us apart in the animal kingdom and makes it possible for us to be rational beings and moral agents.

Reid's fundamental insight was that our ability to make sense of our experience presupposes certain first principles. Because these principles are implicit in our conduct and our thought, they cannot be proven; there are no truths from which they can be derived. However, to deny or even to doubt any of them is to involve ourselves in absurdity. Consequently, the principles of common sense have the special authority of first principles: we cannot operate without them.

As we have noted, according to Reid scientific understanding also presupposes common sense. Leo Strauss makes Reid's point very elegantly in *Natural Right and History*:

> "[T]here is an articulation of reality that precedes all scientific articulation: that articulation, that wealth of meaning, which we have in mind when speaking of the world of common experience or of the natural understanding of the world . . . Since the natural understanding is the presupposition of the scientific understanding, the analysis of science and the world of science presupposes the analysis of the natural understanding, the natural world, or the world of common sense."

What Strauss refers to as the analysis of the natural understanding of the world of common sense is a principle task of the philosopher of common sense.

Reid's use of the term "common sense" is related to, but distinct from, our use of the term in ordinary speech. Reid was aware of the risk of confusion that could result from his decision to put a term from common speech to work as a technical term in philosophy. Nonetheless, he believed it was the right choice for reasons that the Strauss quote helps make clear.

Because Reid included the human capacity to make judgments about what is morally right in his account of common sense, Reid's common sense realism can be said to have encompassed Hutcheson and Smith's concern to make the case for morality—and Reid shared their concern. In his dedication to his great work *An Inquiry into the Human Mind on the Principles of Common*

Sense, Reid portrays himself as motivated to take up his enquiry by moral concern, coming to the defense, as he writes, of "piety, patriotism, friendship, parental affection and private virtue."

F or our purposes the important point is that the Founders were convinced by Hutcheson, Smith, Reid, and their Scottish colleagues. The Founders, in the words of Gordon Wood in his book *The American Revolution,* "identified with Scottish moral or commonsense thinking . . . thereby avoiding "the worst and most frightening implications of Lockean sensationalism."

The Founders used the Scots' account of the moral sense and common sense to conduct what Himmelfarb refers to as their "systematic analysis of the political and social institutions that would promote and protect liberty." The Scots had done the brilliant theoretical work that opened the way for the success of the Founders' systematic analysis and, therefore, for the success of the Founding.

The English Enlightenment of Locke and Newton gave rise to the Scottish Enlightenment which in turn profoundly shaped the American Enlightenment. Meanwhile, the Enlightenments in the English-speaking world were making rapid progress—and in the year 1776 gave us both Adam Smith's *The Wealth of Nations* in Scotland and the Declaration of Independence in America.

THREE

The Declaration of Independence

"All honor to Jefferson—to the man who, in the concrete pressure of a struggle for national independence by a single people, had the coolness, forecast, and capacity to introduce into a merely revolutionary document, an abstract truth, applicable to all men and all times."

—ABRAHAM LINCOLN

JEFFERSON AND LOCKE

*"It has frequently been remarked that Jefferson's philosophy was
thoroughly Lockean, and indeed he did rank Locke as one of 'the
three greatest men that have ever lived, without any exception.'
But we must recall that this same Jefferson also called [Thomas]
Reid's disciple Dugald Stewart one of the two greatest philosophers
of the age, even though Stewart made a career of attacking Locke
for his theory of ideas."*

—JEFFRY MORRISON

This quote is taken from Professor Morrison's important book
John Witherspoon and the Founding of the American Republic.
The book contains a wealth of significant information about the
Founders—and he states the situation accurately. It certainly has
been frequently remarked that Jefferson's philosophy was thor-
oughly Lockean, and Morrison is correct that Jefferson honored
Locke and honored Stewart as described.

However, a problem arises with the use Morrison makes of
this passage. He sees a contradiction here and explains that the
contradiction demonstrates that Jefferson was "inconsistent."

Actually, the fact that Jefferson honored Locke and Stewart
in the way that he did was not a contradiction at all. In honoring
Locke while honoring Stewart and, like Stewart, also being willing
to challenge Locke, Jefferson was simply following a well-estab-
lished tradition of the thinkers of the Scottish Enlightenment. In
the words of Daniel Walker Howe, "the Scots always honored
Locke and considered themselves to be working within his tradition." For example, Reid wrote—high praise!—that Locke "was
no enemy to common sense."

Thomas Reid and his disciple Dugald Stewart were leaders of the philosophical school of common sense realism. They argued that Locke's account of human understanding came up short, and they dedicated themselves to providing an account that would do what was needed. Jefferson was with them all the way, yet he was always even closer in his thinking to Francis Hutcheson. Hutcheson believed that Locke's account did not provide an adequate basis for moral judgments. But Locke had set their tasks for them. Hutcheson, Stewart, and Jefferson saw themselves as working in his tradition. They all, therefore, are Lockeans in that very broad sense.

Locke had set the direction for the Scots and for the Founders. To Locke goes the credit for breaking out of the medieval mindset in which churches and the state colluded, and the state claimed special privileges by divine right. By honoring Locke, studying him, and also by challenging him, the Scots saw themselves as advancing the work that Locke had begun.

The problem with the claim that Jefferson was "thoroughly Lockean" is not only that it creates a contradiction where none exists; the real problem is that it skips from the first chapter of the Enlightenment directly to its glorious culmination, leaving out important developments that shaped the American Founding and made that ultimate chapter such a great and innovative achievement.

Moreover, the belief that Jefferson was "thoroughly Lockean" in his thinking has caused many to overlook the ideas actually at work in the Declaration of Independence.

LOCKE AND THE DECLARATION OF INDEPENDENCE

"The very first sentence of the actual Declaration roundly states that certain truths are—crucial words—self-evident. This style—terse

and pungent, yet fringed with elegance—allied the plain language
of Thomas Paine to the loftier expositions of John Locke . . . "
—CHRISTOPHER HITCHENS, *THOMAS JEFFERSON*

Christopher Hitchens in his 2005 biography of Jefferson observes the tradition of finding the Declaration to be a Lockean document. Although Hitchens was often cheerfully iconoclastic, in this instance he was very much in the mainstream of scholarly and popular comment. It is after all the conventional wisdom that the Declaration is based on the ideas of John Locke.

But is it? If we question this assumption, we encounter big problems right away.

First, there is Locke's definition of "self-evident." Locke's definition would actually disallow the use of those "crucial words" in the Declaration. For Locke, a self-evident truth is a narrowly definitional proposition. In *The Essay Concerning Human Understanding*, Locke offers these examples:

> "a man is a man"; or, "whatsoever is white is white"; or . . . "a man is not a horse"; "red is not blue."

That is, "A=A," or "A≠not-A."

The problem is that the Declaration's self-evident truths do not conform to Locke's definition:

> "We hold these Truths to be self-evident, that all Men are created equal, that they are endowed by their Creator with certain unalienable Rights . . ."

There is a world of difference between Locke's self-evident propositions and the Declaration's self-evident truths. To assert that all men are created equal is to make a claim of a very different kind than the claim that a man is a man. "A man is a man" has the formal structure "A=A," a formal structure that "all men are created equal" does not share. In addition, all "A=A" propositions are perfectly non-controversial, while the Declaration's claim that all men are created equal threw down a challenge to the political order of the whole world of that time, a time when monarchs and nobility possessed political power by right of birth.

Clearly, "all men are created equal" cannot be self-evident according to Locke's definition of self-evidence. Must we then, however reluctantly, admit that the Declaration's claim about equality is really only a way of stating a belief, an opinion? Or can we make sense of the claim that it is a self-evident truth?

Please do not rush past this question. We have heard these words, "We hold these Truths to be self-evident . . ." all our lives. Let us try to grasp the Founders' understanding of self-evident truth here and now for here we approach the very heart of the American Founding. If we seek to understand the Founders, on this point surely we must be clear. As Lincoln said, America is dedicated to the proposition that all men are created equal, "an abstract truth," he wrote, "applicable to all men and all times."

Like the Founders and Lincoln, you and I can understand this self-evident truth in a perfectly straightforward way by means, if you will pardon the expression, of our common sense: it is self-evident that no man is *by nature* the ruler of other men in the way that men are by nature the ruler of horses and cattle. Harry Jaffa in his truly great book *A New Birth of Freedom* puts it like this:

> "That all men are created equal meant, at the very least, that it is a
> fact open to observation by anyone at any time that whatever the
> conventions of any society, human beings are not distinguished

from each other by nature in the way that the rider is distinguished from his horse. The subjection of the horse to the rider is according to nature . . . Nature has made no such distinction between man and man."

When we find a situation in which some men rule over others, that state of affairs cannot arise from the nature of ruler or the nature of the ruled; it must arise from some human arrangement. As Jefferson wrote,

"All eyes are open to or opening to . . . the palpable truth that the mass of mankind has not been born with saddles on their backs, nor a favored few booted and spurred, ready to ride them legitimately, by the grace of God."

Here is Harry Jaffa again, commenting on the Jefferson quote:

"The queen bee is marked out by nature for her function in the hive. Human queens (or kings) are not so marked. Their rule is conventional, not natural. As we have seen Jefferson say, human beings are not born with saddles on their backs, and others booted and spurred to ride them. These are facts accessible to everyone. They are truths that are self-evident."

So we can understand the Founders' claim that it is self-evident that all men are created equal. However, we cannot do so using Locke's definition of "self-evident."

Jefferson was not the only signer of the Declaration who had a thorough knowledge of Locke. There were many others. Yet, to my knowledge, none of the signers objected to the use of "self-evident" in the Declaration because it violated Locke's definition—though of course it did. And they had ample opportunity to object for they made more than eighty amendments to Jefferson's original draft.

That means neither Jefferson nor the other signers of the Declaration were relying on Locke's definition of "self-evident."

Hitchens, of course, does not address this problem. By moving directly to "style" and invoking an alliance with the language of Thomas Paine, he sweeps past it and moves on.

H itchens again finds Locke in the Declaration's proclamation concerning our rights, although, as do many other writers on the Declaration, he does note that "Life, Liberty and the pursuit of Happiness" deviated somewhat from Locke:

> "And where Locke had spoken of 'life, liberty, and property' as being natural rights, Jefferson famously wrote 'life, liberty, and the pursuit of happiness.'"

But setting up the two lists in this way is quite misleading. Hitchens makes it seem that these are two parallel lists, that Jefferson had only changed the last item of a list of three. This version leaves out the most important point. For Locke, property is the overarching concept. Locke puts property front and center:

> "Man . . . hath by nature a power . . . to preserve his property—that is, his life, liberty and estate."

By glossing over the antecedent of Locke's list, Hitchens' parallel creates a false impression.

Let's put Locke's version of the list and the Declaration's version of it in context and side-by-side:

> "Man . . . hath by nature a power . . . to preserve his property—that is, his life, liberty and estate."

> "Men . . . are endowed by their Creator with certain unalienable Rights, . . . among these are Life, Liberty and the pursuit of Happiness."

Locke's triad is appended to property. The Declaration's triad is appended to unalienable rights—and property is missing. With the actual contexts in place, Hitchens' parallel disappears, and we are faced with two fundamentally different accounts.

In fairness to Hitchens, his version is standard fare. Open any book or scholarly paper which discusses the Declaration and you are likely to read that Jefferson "substituted the 'pursuit of happiness' for 'property.'" Part of the problem is that it is all too easy to state it that way. But doing so completely misrepresents the logic of what Jefferson, in crafting the Declaration, did. As Leo Strauss wrote in *Natural Right and History*, "Locke's doctrine of property . . . is almost literally the central part of his political teaching." Here is Locke making the central role of property in his thinking perfectly clear in his *Two Treatises of Government:*

> ". . . the preservation of Property being the end of Government, and that for which Men enter into Society . . ."

Note that for Locke it is not just politics and government that are all about property, but society itself. Yet the Declaration's

"Life, Liberty and the Pursuit of Happiness" not only does not give property Locke's primary role, it omits property altogether.

So far, then, we have the Declaration not following Locke on the meaning of "self-evident" and not following Locke on property as the basis of our rights. In addition, we have "unalienable rights" occupying the space of "property." What is the explanation for all this?

To begin to sort this out, let's start with "self-evident."

I. " . . . SELF-EVIDENT."

What led Hitchens astray? Like other thinkers who have taken the same path, he bypassed the American Enlightenment. Because the American Enlightenment had deep roots in the Scottish Enlightenment, in order to understand the Declaration's use of "self-evident" we first need to turn to the thought of a philosopher of the Scottish Enlightenment—Thomas Reid.

Reid made self-evident truths the foundation of his philosophy, the philosophy of common sense realism. Reidian common sense is the human faculty by means of which we can grasp self-evident truths. It is a power, like Hutcheson's moral sense or the sense of sight or of hearing. Therefore, common sense is the power that makes human understanding possible. The self-evident truths common sense grasps are principles that are implicit in our conduct:

"The same degree of understanding which makes a man capable of acting with common prudence in the conduct of life makes

him capable of discovering what is true and what is false in
matters that are self-evident . . ."

For Reid, self-evident truths are true and discoverable by us
because of the constitution of our human nature.

It is important to understand that Reid was not using common
sense to attack reason; he was attempting to save reason. For
Reid, common sense is the human power of grasping what is
self-evidently true, and therefore the power that makes reason
possible. He argued that without that power we would lack access
to the foundational truths we require to be able to reason, the
axioms necessary for us to be able to reason.

Reid focused on problems within philosophy, problems of
human understanding and human moral understanding. To the
Founders goes the credit for the insights that enabled them to
apply Reid's brilliant philosophical thinking to the political problems they had to confront in order to create America's system
of liberty. The truth that all men are created equal is central to
their new thinking about mankind and the state. Yet there can
be no doubt that the claim that its truth is self-evident relies on
a Reidian understanding of self-evident truth.

R eid wrote that self-evident truths can also be called "first
principles" or "principles of common sense"; they are, he
wrote, "propositions which are no sooner understood than they
are believed . . . [Such a proposition] is not deduced or inferred
from another; it has the light of truth in itself."

Here is Alexander Hamilton putting Reid's understanding of
self-evident truths—or "first principles"—to work, and sounding
very much like Reid while doing so, in *Federalist 31*:

"In disquisitions [discourses] of every kind, there are certain primary truths, or first principles, upon which all subsequent reasonings must depend. These contain an internal evidence which, antecedent to all reflection or combination, commands the assent of the mind."

Hamilton uses Reid's terminology, concepts and manner of thinking to explain and defend the Constitution. At the same time, Hamilton displays how central Reid is to his own thinking.

Madison's mentor, John Witherspoon, was a student of Reid and also probably Reid's most influential champion in America. Consequently, Madison's reliance on Reid is constantly on display. For example, in *Federalist 10*, Madison states a number of propositions which he would have held were self-evident, including the proposition that no man can rightfully be a judge in his own cause. In each instance, he then proceeds in his "subsequent reasonings" by a skillful use of Reidian common sense logic which, Reid taught, transfers the certainty of the original proposition to the conclusion.

"No man is allowed to be a judge in his own cause, because his interest would certainly bias his judgment . . . And what are the different classes of legislators but advocates and parties to the causes which they determine? . . . Yet the parties are, and must be, themselves the judges; and the most numerous party, or, in other words, the most powerful faction must be expected to prevail . . . The inference to which we are brought is, that the *causes* of faction cannot be removed [from government], and that relief is only to be sought in the means of controlling its *effects*." [Italics in the original]

Hamilton and Madison even sound like Reid to the ear.

James Wilson especially always made it clear that he was an exponent of Reid's common sense realism:

> "This philosophy will teach us that first principles are in them-
> selves apparent; that to make nothing self-evident is to take away
> all possibility of knowing anything; that without first principles
> there can be neither reason nor reasoning . . . Consequently,
> all sound reasoning must rest ultimately on the principles of
> common sense."

Wilson wrote of self-evident truths that "though they cannot be proved by reasoning, [they] are known by a species of evidence superior to any that reasoning can produce."

We have just read Hamilton stating the principle of the method, Madison putting the method to work, and Wilson making clear the connection to Reid's philosophy of common sense realism.

Here then is the rock upon which the Founders will build their idea of republican self-government: because a person who is capable of acting with common prudence in the conduct of life is capable of discovering what is true and what is false in matters that are self-evident, self-government is possible.

Hitchens' lack of familiarity with Reid's influence on the thinking of the Founders leads him astray in his discussion of Jefferson and the Declaration. Moreover, his rhetorical linking of Locke and Paine will not stand much scrutiny; Locke, who cautiously supported constitutional monarchy, and Paine, the passionate foe and mocker of monarchy, are just too dissimilar.

Hitchens' rhetorical device does, however, provide an inspired suggestion. If we simply substitute Reid for Locke, Hitchens' formulation works.

Paine, the author of *Common Sense*, and Reid, the author of *An Inquiry into the Human Mind on the Principles of Common Sense*, are natural allies. Hitching a ride on Hitchens' idea, we can say that the Declaration's self-evident truths "allied the plain language of Thomas Paine to the loftier expositions" of Thomas Reid—and we are well on our way to understanding the thinking of the Founders.

II. " . . . UNALIENABLE RIGHTS . . . "

The Declaration proclaims that we have certain "unalienable rights." That *claim* is based on the work of another philosopher of the Scottish Enlightenment—Francis Hutcheson.

Hutcheson's concept of unalienable rights is a direct challenge to Locke's doctrine of property, the core of Locke's political teaching. For Hutcheson, our rights to life and liberty are natural, unalienable, and inherent to our being as humans. What about our right to our property? Here is Hutcheson in *A System of Moral Philosophy*: "Our rights are either alienable or unalienable . . . our right to our goods and labors is naturally alienable." According to Hutcheson, our right to our goods and labors arises out of the division of labor which depends on the right to *exchange* (alienate) them. It is because our right to our property is alienable that we can sell, exchange, and bequeath our property.

Hutcheson's disagreement with Locke is no mere quibble. In the language of the time of the Founders, to alienate is to transfer the title to a property or other right to another person. Here is

David Hume, in a quote I will return to in a few pages, illustrating
the usage of the term in that time:

> "Property shou'd always be stable, except when the proprietor
> agrees to bestow them on some other person. This rule can
> have no ill consequence . . . since the proprietor's consent,
> who alone is concern'd, is taken along in the alienation."

By making the case that our rights to our life and to our liberty
are such that we cannot alienate them, Hutcheson argued that
Locke had not correctly characterized our relationship with those
rights. Property is alienable; unalienable rights are not property.
Our unalienable right to our life and our unalienable right to our
liberty cannot rightfully be sold or transferred as property can
be. According to Hutcheson, our rights to our life and liberty are
inseparable from our nature as rational beings and moral agents.
To say that those rights are unalienable is to emphasize how fundamentally different they are from our right to our property—and
to reject Locke's account.

And to use the phrase "unalienable rights" is to use the language of Hutcheson and his Scottish colleagues. For one example
among a multitude, Reid, following Hutcheson, wrote of "the
natural, the unalienable right of judging for ourselves." Anyone
even slightly familiar with the ideas of Hutcheson and his colleagues will instantly recognize the significance of "unalienable
rights" in the Declaration. It is unmistakable. The Declaration
was with Hutcheson on rights, not with Locke.

There is still more to consider here. Although our right to our
property is naturally alienable, clearly for Hutcheson and

the Founders we have an unalienable right to acquire, possess, and protect property. The Founders' generation understood this distinction and handled it with skill and purpose. This passage in Randy Barnett's book *Restoring the Lost Constitution* makes that clear:

> "Many state constitutions contained similar language. Massachusetts: 'All people are born free and equal, and have certain natural, essential and unalienable rights; among which may be reckoned the right of enjoying and defending their lives and liberties; that of *acquiring, possessing, and protecting property*; in fine, that of seeking and obtaining their safety and happiness.' New Hampshire: 'All men have certain natural, essential, and inherent rights—among which are, the enjoying and defending life and liberty; *acquiring, possessing and protecting property*; and, in a word, of seeking and obtaining happiness.' . . . Vermont: 'That all men are born equally free and independent, and have certain natural, inherent and unalienable rights, amongst which are the enjoying and defending life and liberty; *acquiring, possessing, and protecting property*, and pursuing and obtaining happiness and safety.'" [Italics added by Professor Barnett]

Jefferson's choice to highlight "the Pursuit of Happiness" instead of property in the Declaration, and the quotes from the state constitutions above show clearly that the Founders did not subscribe to Locke's dictum that the preservation of property is the purpose of government. According to the Founders, the legitimate purpose of government is the preservation of our unalienable rights. The Declaration makes that perfectly clear:

". . . that they are endowed by their Creator with certain
unalienable Rights . . . That to secure these Rights, Governments are instituted among Men . . ."

According to the Founders, our rights great and small are
beyond numbering. As James Wilson said in discussing the question of including a bill of rights in the Constitution:

"Enumerate all the rights of men! I am sure, sir, that no gentleman
in the late Convention would have attempted such a thing."

They understood our rights to be literally infinite in number;
there is our right to move freely about the country or stay close to
home, to pursue an occupation of our choice, to start a business,
to invent, to experiment, to innovate, to work hard or to be idle,
to give our all to a noble purpose or choose to live a simple life,
and so on ad infinitum. Hutcheson's account of the foundation of
our rights had opened the way for the Founders' vast new vision of
our rights. The Founders took Hutcheson's account of rights and
ran with it, with the most far-reaching consequences for America.

Here then is the rock upon which the Founders will build
their idea of limited government in crafting the Constitution: because the rightful purpose of government is securing its
citizens' unalienable rights, government is necessarily limited
government, limited because its reach is defined by the vast field
of liberty reserved for the citizens.

One problem with the claim that Jefferson drafted a Lockean
Declaration is that Jefferson first and foremost held to moral

sense doctrine. It is widely recognized that he did. The consequences of that fact are far-reaching, though those scholars who
claim that the Declaration is Lockean hold back from drawing
the obvious conclusion. To hold as Jefferson did to moral sense
doctrine was to follow Hutcheson. Jefferson was a master of
Hutcheson's challenge to Locke's claim that our rights are our
property, and that mastery is perfectly revealed in the second
paragraph of the Declaration, the paragraph which contains the
proclamation concerning our rights.

One problem with the claim that the Founders were Lockeans
is the fact that the second paragraph of the Declaration, as drafted
by Jefferson, was left virtually untouched by the other delegates.
They did not correct it to bring it into alignment with Locke. To
make matters worse for the champions of the Lockean Declaration, the state constitutions quoted above by Professor Barnett
show the same familiarity with, and mastery of, Hutcheson's
challenge to Locke. A glance at them makes it perfectly clear that
Hutcheson's influence on the Founders was pervasive. Instead of
seizing the opportunity to rally around Locke's doctrine of rights
as property, these state constitutions reinforce "unalienable rights."
They declare that our unalienable rights are also "natural", "essential", and "inherent." Instead of explaining our rights in terms of
property, the state constitutions claim that our right to acquire,
possess, and protect property is properly understood to be one of
our unalienable rights. We find the influence of Hutcheson all the
way down the line.

Jefferson claimed that he was speaking for the Founders in the
Declaration, as he explained in an often quoted letter to Henry
Lee in 1825. The purpose of the Declaration of Independence,
he wrote, was:

"Not to find out new principles, or new arguments, never before thought of . . . but to place before mankind the common sense of the subject . . . it was intended to be an expression of the American mind."

That is precisely what Jefferson succeeded in doing.

We should note an important consequence of the Founders' belief that the people could not rightfully and did not in fact alienate their unalienable rights when they established the federal government; it was the source of their principled opposition to including a bill of rights in the Constitution. Madison and many other Founders initially opposed the idea. Here is Hamilton in *Federalist 84*:

"It has been several times truly remarked, that bills of rights are, in their origin, stipulations between kings and their subjects, abridgments of prerogative in favour of privilege . . . Such was the MAGNA CHARTA, obtained by the barons, sword in hand, from King John . . . Such, also, was the Declaration of Right presented by the Lords and Commons to the Prince of Orange in 1688, and afterwards thrown into the form of an act of Parliament called the Bill of Rights. It is evident, therefore, that they have no application to constitutions, professedly founded upon the power of the people . . . Here, in strictness, the people surrender nothing; and as they retain everything they have no need of particular reservations . . . For why declare that things shall not be done which there is no power to do? Why, for instance, should it be said that the liberty of

the press shall not be restrained, when no power is given by
which restrictions may be imposed?"

The difference between British constitutionalism and the American Constitution is here made clear. In the American idea, we
possess certain unalienable rights, and those unalienable rights
inherently limit government power. For Madison and Hamilton,
a bill of rights, traditionally a concession of privileges wrested
from the sovereign political power, had no place in the American
Constitution.

When Madison eventually realized that the public's demand
for a bill of rights made it a political necessity, he took responsibility for drafting it, and made certain it included the Ninth
Amendment:

"The enumeration in the Constitution, of certain rights, shall not
be construed to deny or disparage others retained by the people."

The Ninth was intended to insure that enumerating some rights
would not have the effect of narrowing our understanding of the
vast range of our unalienable rights.

We are now in a position to note that Hutcheson's brilliant
analysis of alienable rights and unalienable rights was
astonishingly fruitful. It provided the intellectual foundation for
two of the greatest achievements in world history, *The Wealth of
Nations* and the Declaration of Independence.

We have seen the importance of Hutcheson's concept of
unalienable rights to the thinking of Jefferson, John Adams (those

are his words in the Massachusetts Constitution quoted above), and the other Founders. In addition, Hutcheson, you will recall, was Adam Smith's mentor, and Hutcheson's analysis of the alienability of property opened the way for Smith's world-changing achievement, *The Wealth of Nations.* We will turn to a consideration of *Wealth* further on, but let us here briefly note that in it Smith famously demonstrated that the division of labor is the source of the wealth of nations. In one of the most frequently quoted passages from *Wealth,* Smith makes clear the source of the all-important division of labor:

> "This division of labour . . . is the necessary . . . consequence of a certain propensity in human nature . . . ; the propensity to truck, barter, and exchange one thing for another."

We can "truck, barter, and exchange" because our right to our property is, as Hutcheson showed, naturally alienable.

1776, the year of *The Wealth of Nations* and the Declaration of Independence, marks the economic and political boundary between the world in which you and I live and all that went before. Our debt to Hutcheson by way of Smith and the Founders is beyond reckoning.

III. " . . . AND THE PURSUIT OF HAPPINESS."

Those who contend that the Declaration is Lockean usually offer one explanation or another for the fact that the Declaration gives pride of place to the pursuit of happiness instead of property. But this much is obvious: Jefferson, by drafting it so that it did not give primacy to property, and the other delegates, by approving Jefferson's draft, were not following Locke.

However, giving primacy to the pursuit of happiness in the Declaration does echo Hutcheson. Here is Hutcheson: "the general happiness is the supreme end [the purpose] of all political union." This is a direct contradiction of Locke's claim that the preservation of property is the end (the purpose) of government.

In addition, it is important to note that Hutcheson had made happiness a core concern of the Scottish Enlightenment, and, therefore, of the American Enlightenment. For example, here is Adam Smith, following Hutcheson, in his book *The Theory of Moral Sentiments*:

> "All constitutions of government, however, are valued only in proportion as they tend to promote the happiness of those who live under them."

Here is James Wilson in a pamphlet published in 1774 in which he too follows Hutcheson on happiness. In addition, Wilson demonstrates just how closely the Founders linked the concept of happiness with their radical new concept of liberty:

> "All men are, by nature, equal and free: no one has a right to any authority over another without his consent: all lawful government is founded on the consent of those who are subject to it . . . The consequence is, that the happiness of the society is the *first* law of every government." [Emphasis in the original]

Social happiness (which Washington mentions in the very first quotation cited at the beginning of this book) was a much-considered concern of the Founders, and each of the state constitutions quoted above declared our unalienable right to pursue happiness.

Because Hitchens was evidently unaware of this deep background, he seemed to imagine that the phrase was newly-minted by Jefferson:

> "'the pursuit of happiness' belongs to that limited group of lapidary phrases that has changed history, and it seems that the delegates realized this as soon as they heard it."

Actually, the phrase was a central element of what Jefferson referred to as "the common sense of the subject" and "an expression of the American mind." According to the Founders, government's legitimate purpose of preserving our unalienable rights has a social test—the happiness of the society the government serves. All men are by nature equal and free, and only a government based on recognizing that foundational truth can meet the test of happiness.

IV. " . . . ALL MEN ARE CREATED EQUAL . . . "

We now arrive at the very core of the American Idea—only to be greeted, once again, by Francis Hutcheson. Here he is discussing equality in *A System of Moral Philosophy*:

> "*The natural equality of men* consists chiefly in this, that these natural rights belong equally to all . . . Had providence intended that some men should have a perfect right to govern the rest without their consent, we should have had as visible undisputed marks distinguishing these rulers from others as

3

clearly as the human shape distinguishes men from beasts."
[Italics in the original]

No doubt the longer part of this quote reminds you of the Jefferson passage quoted earlier on, the one about the "truth that the mass of mankind has not been born with saddles on their backs, nor a favored few booted and spurred." Of course you are correct. One of Jefferson's greatest gifts was his ability to state the ideas of others better, more gracefully, and more memorably than they could.

So far in our examination of the Declaration it has not gone well for the claim that the Declaration is a Lockean document. But Locke is in the Declaration—only not where Hitchens thought he found him. And where Locke is found makes all the difference for understanding the Declaration.

The "long train of abuses" section is often cited as proof that the Declaration is a Lockean document. Here is that passage as it appeared in Jefferson's original draft:

> "But when a long train of abuses and usurpations, begun at a distinguished period and pursuing invariably the same object, evinces a design to reduce them under absolute despotism it is their right, it is their duty, to throw off such government . . ."

And here is the parallel section in Locke's *Second Treatise*.

> "But if a long train of abuses, Prevarications, and Artifices, all tending the same way, make the design visible to the people, and they cannot but feel, what they lie under, and see, whither

they are going: 'tis not to be wonder'd, that they should then
rouze themselves, and endeavor to put the rule into such hands,
which may secure to them the ends for which Government was
first erected . . ."

However, noting the likeness of the two passages actually does
much less for the proponents of the Lockean Declaration than
they claim for it. Scholars who point to the parallel and declare
that they have found Locke in the Declaration are missing Jefferson's point. Jefferson wanted his readers, especially his readers
in Britain, to notice he was virtually quoting Locke; he wanted
them to notice because he was putting Locke to work against
the British. Locke's long train of abuses section justifies Britain's
Glorious Revolution. Jefferson's long train of abuses section justifies the American Revolution.

You could say those scholars just mentioned don't get Jefferson's
joke. With irreverent wit, Jefferson skillfully invoked Locke's very
great authority and Britain's history against George III. Jefferson
cleverly used Locke to advance the cause of the American Revolution, and, incidentally, greatly improved Locke's prose while he
was at it. Thanks to Jefferson, the Founders defied the world's
greatest military power with wit and style.

Those same scholars also generally overlook how devastating
the Locke passage is to their larger claim that the Declaration is
a Lockean document. Let's take another look at how the Locke
quote concludes:

". . . endeavor to put the rule into such hands, which may
secure to them the ends for which Government was first
erected . . ."

Putting "the rule into such hands" meant finding a different monarch to rule them, which is what the Glorious Revolution accomplished. Locke's long train of abuses section justified Britain finding a new monarch to rule the British. Surely there is no need to make the point that Jefferson and the Founders were not in the market for a new and improved king to rule America on more acceptable terms.

Here is another comparison. The Declaration:

> "Prudence indeed will dictate that governments long established should not be changed for light and transient cause; and accordingly all experience hath shown that mankind are more *disposed to suffer* while evils are sufferable than to *right themselves* by abolishing the forms to which they are accustomed."

Locke:

> "For till the mischief be grown general, and the ill designs of the Rulers become visible, or their attempts sensible to the greater part, the People, who are more *disposed to suffer*, than *right themselves* by Resistance, are not apt to stir."

I have highlighted "disposed to suffer" and "right themselves" to draw out the likeness that exists. Once again there is an important difference though. The Declaration's "abolishing the forms to which they are accustomed" points to that difference: the Americans intended to go far beyond deciding "to stir" themselves and put their rule into new, more acceptable hands.

What then can we say in a general way about the use Jefferson made of Locke in the Declaration? As Lincoln made clear in his words introducing this chapter, the Declaration has two parts, the "revolutionary document" and the "abstract truth" portion:

> "All honor to Jefferson . . . who . . . had the coolness, forecast, and capacity to introduce into a merely revolutionary document, an abstract truth, applicable to all men and all times."

Jefferson put Locke, the champion of the Glorious Revolution, to work in the revolutionary document. Nothing could be more appropriate. After all, Locke had made the case for the people's right to resist tyranny and replace their ruler with a new one.

But Jefferson went far beyond justifying the American Revolution in Lockean terms. He introduced the universal principles which would, within a few years after the American victory, guide the Framers of the Constitution. So guided, they would create an entirely new *form of government* unprecedented in the history of the world. "All men are created equal" would result in government by, for, and of the people.

That new form of government cannot be found in Locke. Nor can it be found in Reid or in Hutcheson. But learning from Reid and Hutcheson, as we have seen, puts us on the right track to understand Jefferson's immortal statement of the Declaration's universal principles, the principles upon which the Founders were to build their new creation.

One final point of special emphasis: that all men are created equal does not mean that everyone has the same talents or interests or intelligence. Obviously, men of such astonishing gifts and accomplishments as Jefferson and Lincoln could not possibly have meant that. They meant all men are born equal in rights. They were rejecting the idea that there could be one law for the king, another for the ruling class, and yet another for everyone else. Here is how Ludwig von Mises put it in his essay "On Equality and Inequality":

> "The doctrine of natural law that inspired the eighteenth century declarations of the rights of man did not imply the obviously fallacious proposition that all men are biologically equal. It proclaimed that all men are born equal in rights and that this equality cannot be abrogated by any man-made law."

THE AMERICAN IDEA OF PROPERTY

"Those who founded the United States of America and wrote the Constitution saw property rights as essential for safeguarding all other rights. *The right to free speech, for example, would be mean-ingless if criticisms of the authorities could lead to whatever you owned being seized in retaliation . . . Property rights are legal barriers to politicians, judges or bureaucrats arbitrarily seizing the assets of some human beings to transfer those assets to other human beings." [Emphasis added]*
—THOMAS SOWELL, INTELLECTUALS AND SOCIETY

"Property systems open to all citizens are a relatively recent phe-nomenon—no more than two hundred years old."
—HERNANDO DE SOTO, THE MYSTERY OF CAPITAL

In order to secure our unalienable right to pursue, acquire, use, and alienate property, Americans needed to come up with a new property system for the new nation. The system they came up with differed in important ways from the system that was the background for Locke's thinking—and it laid the foundation for the unprecedented prosperity that is part of the American story almost from the beginning.

For the Founders, the purpose of government is to protect our rights, and the American concept of property shared that primary concern. As Thomas Sowell makes clear, the American system of strong property rights is a safeguard of all other rights. The Americans grasped that early on. In addition, the American concept of property focused on the alienability of property. In the American idea, strong property rights and alienability go hand-in-hand.

Initially, the colonists had attempted to rely on English property law. However, they soon found, in the words of the economist Hernando De Soto, that

> "the English common law of property was often ill suited to deal with the problems that confronted the colonists . . . Americans built a new concept of property,' one that emphasized its dynamic aspects, associating it with economic growth . . . American property changed from being a means of preserving an old economic order to being, instead, a powerful tool for creating a new one."

A property system rooted in feudal England did not fit American circumstances or the American character. England's great estates were kept in one piece by primogeniture and entail, restrictions on inheritance which together ensured that the entire property was inherited by a single heir. The vast inherited wealth of the aristocracy played a central role in preserving the English political and social order. The brilliant political thinker and influential Member of Parliament Edmund Burke gives us a sense of that in a letter he wrote to the Duke of Richmond in 1772:

> "You people of great families and hereditary trusts and fortunes are not like such as I am, who, whatever may be the rapidity of our growth, and even by the fruit we bear, and flatter ourselves a little that, while we creep on the ground, we belly into melons that are exquisite for size and flavor, yet still we are but annual plants that perish with our season, and leave no sort of traces behind us. You, if you are what you ought to be, are in my eye the great oaks that shade a country, and perpetuate your benefits from generation to generation."

Not just great wealth, but also inherited political power and privilege were the property of the family, to be passed down to each generation. This family-centered concept of property, assuming as it does a static world of aristocratic inequality, had roots deep in antiquity. Larry Siedentop reminds us of this in his fascinating book *Inventing the Individual*:

> "In the earliest Greek and Roman law, the sale of property was virtually forbidden. And even in later, historical ages such a sale was surrounded by prohibitions and penalties . . . property belonged not to an individual man, but to the family. The eldest male possessed the land as a trust."

During early Greek and Roman times distributing property upon death by means of a will was unknown. When it was eventually permitted in Athens, it was only allowed for the childless.

In England, as in ancient Greece and Rome, restrictions on inheritance and land conveyance kept the economic and political order frozen in place to the benefit of the aristocratic families, as they were intended to do. In America there was not going be an aristocracy, and America was not going to follow the English example by having primogeniture or entail either. Jefferson and Madison detested primogeniture and entail, and after the Revolution they went to work to rid America of every vestige of them. In this as in so much else they were agreeing with and also following Adam Smith.

Unburdened by a feudal past, the Americans innovated. America's "dynamic new concept of property" was fashioned into a "powerful tool for creating a new economic order." The American property system was open to all citizens. Strong property rights and clear titles promoted the alienability of property, creating the conditions for economic dynamism.

The Americans understood that American liberty required that every farmer and every property owner have a clear title to their property. Consequently, America set out on a multi-generational enterprise to survey America's hundreds of millions of acres, eventually establishing clear title to it all. The enormous scale of the task and the central role it played in the life of the nation well into the nineteenth century can be glimpsed in the fact that both Washington and Lincoln in their early years worked as surveyors.

Doing away with the limitations on the transfer of property that had favored the aristocracy was not the most important element of America's new concept of property. More important was the fact that Americans also created conditions favoring the transfer of property among ordinary citizens. That is what De Soto found when he examined American economic history in order to find out what had set America apart from the rest of the world. He found the answer in strong property rights grounded in clear titles to property. Third World countries today, he notes, have failed to follow America's example in carrying out this fundamental task. They lack property systems open to all people. Informal land tenure is still the norm in developing countries. De Soto makes the case that this fact, more than any other, explains the failure of those countries to emerge from poverty. Informal tenure promotes poverty by suppressing the economic potential of property. It severely restricts the transfer—the alienation—of property. It also prevents using property to obtain affordable secured credit, and inhibits investment because of the risk of uncompensated takings.

The American concept of property is an essential part of the story of how America, itself once an undeveloped nation, became the economic dynamo of the whole world. De Soto's research into American economic history shows that the evolution of the American property system has been a neglected area of historical research. At this point in the study of this important part of the American story, however, we are in a position to make this observation: the innovative process that brought it into being was very much a spontaneous one, growing out of the unique American character, the ideas of the American Enlightenment, and America's unique circumstances.

The Scots can again come to our aid in understanding this remarkable story. The Scottish Enlightenment philosopher Adam Ferguson provided an analysis of how the most basic human institutions come to be. They are, he wrote, "the result of human action, but not the execution of any human design." They evolve, arising by the process of trial and error conducted by many people dispersed over space and acting over the generations.

Ferguson's paradigm is the perfect tool for understanding the evolution of the American property system. Many individual actions, legal decisions and choices by groups and governing bodies all contributed to crafting it—yet no one was responsible for coordinating the process. In this remarkable evolutionary process, Americans relied on their common sense and their moral sense, their sense of what is right and wrong, as they made their way forward in a vast cooperative enterprise, extended over space and time, resulting in a fundamentally new way of conducting the project of living and working together. Because it emerged in this way it has often failed to catch the attention of historians.

Clear titles and strong property rights are essential to the American idea because they provide the individual citizen with a secure base from which to conduct the responsibilities of citizenship. They also confer many other benefits, both to the individual and to society, not least by promoting social harmony and prosperity. Adam Smith's close friend David Hume could have been writing for any of his Scottish colleagues or any of the Founders when he wrote:

> "Property shou'd always be stable, except when the proprietor agrees to bestow them on some other person. This rule can have no ill consequence . . . since the proprietor's consent, who alone is concern'd, is taken along in the alienation: And it may serve to many good purposes in adjusting properties to persons . . . different men both are by nature fitted for different employments, and attain to greater perfection in any one, when they confine themselves to it alone. All this requires a mutual exchange and commerce; for which reason the translation of property by consent is founded on a law of nature."

The American innovation was to take the steps, great and small, legal and practical, required to extend these benefits highlighted by Hume far and wide. The economist Ludwig von Mises, in his very great book *Liberalism*, makes the point this way in his very first words in that book:

> "The social order created by the philosophy of the Enlighten-ment assigned supremacy to the common man. In his capacity as a consumer, the "regular fellow" was called upon to deter-mine ultimately what should be produced, in what quantity, and of what quality, by whom, how, and where; in his capacity as a voter, he was sovereign in directing the nation's policies."

As Mises well understood, the American Enlightenment was at the center of this revolutionary change to the economic, political, and social order that made the modern world.

FOUR

The Constitution

"The powers delegated by the proposed Constitution to the federal government are few and defined. Those which are to remain in the State governments are numerous and indefinite. The former will be exercised principally on external objects, as war, peace, negotiation, and foreign commerce . . . The powers reserved to the several States will extend to all the objects which, in the ordinary course of affairs, concern the lives, liberties, and properties of the people, and the internal order, improvement, and prosperity of the State."
—JAMES MADISON, *FEDERALIST 45*

UNDERSTANDING MADISON

"Madison's political feelings were most aroused, oddly enough, not by the imperial issues of trade and taxation . . . it was the union of Church and State that set him on fire. The cause of religious freedom became Madison's passport to revolution."
—MERRILL PETERSON, *JAMES MADISON: A BIOGRAPHY IN HIS OWN WORDS*

For Madison, there was, of course, nothing odd here. Madison simply is the great champion of religious liberty. That fact is the key to understanding his political thought in general. Yet Madison's focus on religious liberty strikes Prof. Peterson as odd. Why?

The problem is that Madison's great central passion does not fit the reigning narrative in academia. The academic narrative tends to favor economic and political explanations and to down-play explanations involving religion. It is better for the standard narrative if he is seen as focused on the "imperial issues of trade and taxation." But Madison cannot be made to conform to the paradigm Prof. Peterson prefers.

Madison was educated at Princeton where, under the leader-ship of John Witherspoon, religious liberty was both practiced and defended. On his return to his native Virginia, he was "set on fire" when Baptist preachers were imprisoned at the behest of Virginia's established church, the Anglican Church. This event was the catalyst of Madison's decision to enter politics.

Religious liberty was even the focus of Madison's very first foray into constitution-making.

At the age of 25 in 1776, Madison was a newly-elected del-egate appointed to the committee to prepare a constitution and a declaration of rights for Virginia. Because of his youth and junior status, he kept a very low profile on the committee—until the work on the declaration of rights came to the issue of religious conscience. George Mason, who dominated the committee's proceedings, proposed "the fullest Toleration in the exercise of religion." In the words of Prof. Peterson:

> "The concept of toleration, as in the English Toleration Act previously in force in the colony [of Virginia] and in Locke's celebrated *Letter Concerning Toleration*, assumed an official and preferred religion along with the right of the State to grant or to withhold favor from 'dissenting' religions."

But toleration did not go nearly far enough for Madison, and Mason's proposal aroused him to action. He proposed instead that religious liberty be declared, in his words, "a natural and absolute right."

Madison's formulation carried the day in Virginia and, as the result of his untiring efforts, in America as well. We can see this very clearly in Washington's celebrated "Letter to the Hebrew Congregation in Newport" of 1790:

> "The citizens of the United States of America have . . . given to mankind examples of a . . . policy worthy of imitation. All possess alike liberty of conscience . . . It is now no more that toleration is spoken of . . . "

Here Washington declares that the new vision of liberty of conscience Madison successfully championed in America is a gift to mankind.

Madison, you see, was a true revolutionary. The Revolution for him was not simply a matter of replacing the Colonial government with a new, indigenous government in order to address issues of taxation and trade and, like the Virginia colony, enact its own Toleration Act. The Bill of Rights makes this clear. Drafted by Madison, it forbade Congress even to legislate about an established religion. America was not going to have an official and preferred religion. Here are the first ten words of the Bill of Rights, as found in the First Amendment:

> "Congress shall make no law respecting an establishment of religion . . ."

Madison was fighting for a radical re-conception of the relationship of mankind and the state. For Madison, liberty of conscience is a natural and unalienable right of the individual.

And, according to the Founders, so it is for all of our rights. The eminent philosopher Daniel Robinson got it just right in his brilliant paper "Do the people of the United States form a nation?"

> "The rights in question are not the gift of enlightened government nor an offshoot of the Magna Carta, nor some sort of compact or social contract. The rights were there all along, and no government can claim validity or authenticity or the fidelity of the governed unless it is based on just this recognition."

"The rights were there all along." That is to say, our rights are inherent, part of our nature as human beings, unalienable.

In order to understand the Founders, we need to recognize their intent: to design America's government guided by this new understanding of the nature of our rights, and, insofar as possible, to design government so as to protect and preserve those rights.

O ne more point: today the First Amendment is being used to drive religion out of public life. The Founders would consider that absurd and repellent. The plain meaning of the First Amendment is that there is not going to be a Church of America. The Founders assumed that the United States would be filled with churches of many denominations, and they believed that for America to thrive those churches needed to thrive also. Here is John Adams, speaking in 1798: "Our constitution is made only for a moral and religious people. It is wholly inadequate to the government of any other."

ON HUMAN NATURE

"If men were angels, no government would be necessary. If angels were to govern men, neither external nor internal controls on government would be necessary."
—JAMES MADISON, *FEDERALIST 51*

"That 'all men are created equal' means not only that all men have been equally endowed with certain rights by their Creator but also that they have been endowed by that same Creator with a nonangelic nature."
—HARRY JAFFA, *A NEW BIRTH OF FREEDOM*

"The Scottish theorists were very much aware how delicate this artificial structure of civilization was which rested on man's more primitive and ferocious instincts . . . They were very far from

holding such naïve views . . . as the 'natural goodness of man,'
or the existence of a 'natural harmony of interests' . . . [They]
showed how certain institutional arrangements would induce man
to use his intelligence to the best effect and how institutions could
be framed so that bad people could do least harm."
—F. A. HAYEK, *THE CONSTITUTION OF LIBERTY*

The Founders were committed to government by, for and of the people, but like the thinkers of the Scottish Enlightenment they were under no illusions about human nature. As Jefferson said, "let no more be heard of confidence in man, but bind him down from mischief by the chains of the Constitution."

If we want to understand the efforts of the Framers during that hot summer in 1787, we must see them as trying to design self-government with a sober assessment of human nature in mind. When in the next century Lord Acton wrote "power tends to corrupt, and absolute power corrupts absolutely," he captured in a ringing aphorism the view of the Founders.

This understanding of the effect of political power on human nature explains the Framers' focus on defining and limiting federal power. They did so by distributing power among the executive, legislative and judicial branches of the federal government, preserving the political independence of the states and creating a zone of liberty around the individual—even by further dividing the (supreme) legislative power itself, crafting two legislative bodies with separate powers and potentially competing interests. Jefferson put it this way:

"What has destroyed liberty and the rights of man in every government which has ever existed under the sun? The generalizing and concentrating all cares and powers into one body."

And Lord Acton put it this way:

> "Liberty consists in the division of power. Absolutism, in con-
> centration of power."

The Framers of the Constitution aimed to preserve our unalienable rights by preventing the concentration of political power.

Put yourself for a moment in the place of one of the Framers.
Imagine that it is your responsibility to craft a government
whereby the people will govern themselves. And, just for the
moment, also imagine that you are, like the Framers, under no
illusions about the natural goodness of man. Now, how do you
define your challenge?

Hayek's contemporary, the philosopher Karl Popper offered
a statement of the task of making a government that, I believe,
illuminates the wisdom of the Framers. He proposed that if we
face *from the beginning* the possibility of bad government, the
question then becomes "how can we so organize political institutions that bad or incompetent rulers can be prevented from
doing too much damage?" And that is just how the Framers
approached their task.

The great tragedy of the modern world is that France did not
follow the example of the Americans. The French opted for
unlimited popular sovereignty instead of limited government, and
for that they paid a terrible price. In doing so, they were not following Voltaire, but Voltaire's younger contemporary, Jean-Jacques
Rousseau. (Neither Voltaire nor Rousseau lived to see the revolution they did so much to define. It began in 1789; both men died
in 1778.) Rousseau's starting point was that man is by nature good.
The political doctrine he arrived at was the concept of "the general

will." The general will did not provide for individual rights, for property rights (he said the first man who fenced a cabbage patch should have been put to death), or for the rights of the minority. In Rousseau's political vision, everyone surrenders all their rights and submits to the general will which then creates and maintains absolute equality. Freedom in society is achieved by total submission to society. Everyone and everything must be subject to the general will. What is required, as he wrote, was "the total alienation of each associate, with all his rights, to the whole community."

There is that word "alienation" again. The stand their political leaders took on whether or not we have unalienable rights made a very consequential difference to the people of America and the people of France. According to Rousseau, if the leaders decide that "it is expedient for the state" that a citizen die, that citizen should die. In the grip of Rousseau's vision of the alienation of all rights in the service of equality, the French Revolution of 1789 quickly descended into the blood-drenched Terror, and despotism even worse than the one the Revolution had overthrown. As Paul Johnson writes in his biography of Napoleon,

> "the Revolution left behind . . . an absolute concentration of
> authority, first in parliament, then in a committee, finally in a
> single tyrant, that had never been known before; and a universal
> teaching that such concentration expressed *the general will of
> a united people.*" [Emphasis added]

During the frantic period between Louis XVI and Napoleon, French citizens in the thousands were sent to the guillotine by the people who ruled France. They were the victims of politics run amok.

Inevitably, the concentration of political power soon enough devolved into the government Voltaire and Diderot had favored all along, the despotism of a "reforming monarch." Napoleon established a military dictatorship with all power held by one person. In the words of Paul Johnson:

> "In fact, the new First Consul [Napoleon] was far more powerful than Louis XIV, since he dominated the armed forces directly in a country that was now organized as a military state. All the ancient legal restraints on divine-right kingship—the church, the aristocracy and its resources, the courts, the cities and their charters, the universities and their privileges, the guilds and their immunities—all had already been swept away by the Revolution . . ."

Tragically for Europe and the world, it was the French Revolution instead of the American Revolution that set the terms of political debate thereafter in Europe. The French Revolution provided the prototype of the political revolutions of the modern era, and Napoleonic France provided the prototype of the modern war-making totalitarian state, the full potentialities of which were to be realized in the twentieth century.

It was also the tragic destiny of France to create the model of the modern perversion of self-government, the evil twin of the Founders' creation, and to bequeath it to posterity. Like Hitler, Napoleon gained power through a series of plebiscites. Sophia Rosenfeld in her book *Common Sense* describes his accomplishment succinctly:

> "Napoleon's great innovation . . . was to keep alive the idea of unlimited popular sovereignty . . . in the service of the

curtailment of individual liberty and his own personal seizure
of power. He successfully mobilized 'the people' in support of
policies that disempowered them."

His elevation to Emperor in 1804 was overwhelmingly approved
by a vote of France's citizens in a constitutional referendum.

Rousseau's doctrine of the general will justified equally Napoleon's despotism and the chaotic period that preceded it. What
those two periods had in common, and what they had in common
with the absolute monarchy by divine right they had replaced,
was absolutism.

A merica took a different path. America's constitutional referendum ratified the Constitution, our charter of liberty and
self-government, instead of installing an Emperor of America.
The Revolutionary War won, Washington did not seize power, as
many in Europe assumed he would.

In London, George III asked the American-born painter Benjamin West what Washington, having won the war, would do. West
replied that it was said he would return to his farm. "If he does
that," said the king, "he will be the greatest man in the world."

Washington did that, and he was.

Peace concluded, Washington resigned his military commission and went home to Mount Vernon and private life in 1783,
astonishing the world. He returned to public life to preside
over the Constitutional Convention in 1787, and to public office
when he was elected President in 1789. He served two terms as
president, each time winning every vote of the Electoral College.
He then again astonished the world by declining to serve a third,

leaving office in 1797 and retiring to Mount Vernon, a private citizen once more.

THE VIEW FROM WINDSOR CASTLE

"George III was not far wrong . . . when he called the [American] Revolution "a Presbyterian Rebellion."
—PAUL JOHNSON, *A HISTORY OF THE AMERICAN PEOPLE*

We have seen that the wave of Scots, Presbyterians all, who came to America during the colonial era shaped the thinking of the Founders. But King George did more than blame those Scots for inciting rebellion among his American subjects. He took aim at a specific Scottish institution as the real source of the trouble, an institution that had vexed so many monarchs before him— the Presbyterian Church, called "the Kirk" by the Scots.

John Knox, the Martin Luther of the Scottish Reformation, founded the Presbyterian Church in 1560-1561. Long before the Founders began to make their argument for popular sovereignty, Knox preached popular sovereignty as a matter of doctrine. Political authority, Knox taught and the Presbyterians believed, ultimately belonged to the people. According to Knox, the people had the right to choose those who would manage their political affairs, and it was the people's right to remove them at will. Knox famously treated the sequence of monarchs with whom he had to deal during his lifetime with undisguised impatience and contempt, and the Kirk was often at odds with the monarchy. As Lord Acton wrote in his magisterial *Essays in the History of Liberty*, "Scotland was the only kingdom in which the Reformation triumphed over the resistance of the State." The triumph of Knox and the Kirk was to have the profoundest of consequences for America's Founding.

Hitchhiking on King George's insight, we are in a position to understand that John Knox's enormous influence had already set the direction for the Scots when they entered the great philosophical project of the eighteenth century and began to work out their own version of the Enlightenment. Subsequently, the Founders learned from the Scots and applied those ideas to the great task of creating a representative system of government for America.

Even the Kirk itself offered a model of such a government, and it was a model that offered precisely the features Madison was looking for.

The Kirk had from the beginning a representative system of government. As Arthur Herman describes it in his fascinating book *How the Scots Invented the Modern World*:

> "Even the minister was chosen by the congregation's consistory of elected elders . . . The elders also sent representatives to their local synod, who in turn sent representatives to the Kirk's General Assembly. This meant that the members of the Kirk's governing body really were representatives of the people."

Both the doctrine of popular sovereignty and a functioning representative governing body that embodied the doctrine of popular sovereignty were unique to Scotland during that time.

Two centuries later the Founders fought a revolution to establish the right of popular sovereignty in America. Then, when it came time to design a system of government by and for the people, James Madison proposed a design that bears a remarkable, though generally unnoticed, resemblance to the Presbyterian system. Called "the Virginia Plan," it was the original proposal written by Madison and presented by Edmund Randolph at the Constitutional Convention. This initial proposal opened the discussion and became the basis of the debate. David O. Stewart in his book *The Summer of 1787* describes the Virginia Plan like this:

> "The people would elect the 'first Branch' of the legislature . . . That 'first branch' (the future House of Representatives) would choose the 'second branch' (the future Senate). Together, those two houses would select the president and appoint all the judges."

Although the Virginia plan has been the subject of much scholarly discussion, its striking resemblance to the Kirk's system of representative government is consistently overlooked. Yet it is a fact worthy of note that Madison initiated the Constitutional debate with a plan that could have been taken directly from Scottish, even Presbyterian, history.

Though it is remarkable, it is not inexplicable. We know that Madison was steeped in the Scottish tradition. Princeton, his alma mater, had been founded by the Presbyterians to provide for the education of their American clergy. Because of Madison's involvement with what Garry Wills calls the "Princeton/Presbyterian network," we know that Madison was very familiar with the workings of the Presbyterian ministry. Wills writes:

> "In his close circle of friends at the school were several who entered, or considered entering, the Presbyterian ministry, and he admired and kept in touch with them for years . . . Madison

even went to Philadelphia in 1774, when the Presbyterians' annual synod was taking place, to see the friends assembling there."

Madison's problem, and the Founders' problem, was finding a design for representative government that was likely to succeed and endure. It would have been very much in character for Madison to propose something like the Presbyterian system. After all, that system was at hand, had been tested by experience and had stood the test of time.

An important feature of the Presbyterian model for Madison would surely have been the fact that the people and their elected representatives populated the government all the way to the top. The problem with the British model was that the House of Lords was in the hands of the hereditary nobility and the executive was in the hands of the hereditary monarch. Since America was not going to have a king and it was not going to have a House of Lords, there was no way to make the British model fit America's needs.

In our desire to understand America's Founding, we do well to take note of the fact that we find both the doctrine of popular sovereignty and a working model of the system of representative government in Reformation Scotland—more than two centuries before the American Revolution.

It is all too easy for us today to fail to recognize how much of Madison's proposed system of representation actually made it into the Constitution of 1787. This is because the original system of federal elections was significantly different from the one we have today. Only the way we now elect the members of the House is according to the original Constitution.

According to Madison's Virginia Plan, the voters would only directly elect the members of the first branch. The Constitution of 1787 preserved that basic feature. Members of the House of Representatives were the only federal officers directly elected by the voters. The indirect election of U.S. senators was also carried over from the Virginia Plan to the Constitution. U.S. senators were elected by each state legislature; the state legislatures did the selecting in place of Madison's first branch. This followed Madison's proposed format of indirect representation for the upper chamber with the additional advantage of also providing the states representation within the federal government.

This modification of Madison's original plan by the Framers was brilliant. Having the first branch of the federal legislature choose the second branch would have had the effect of binding the two branches close together. The selection of senators would also have been a collective process by the first branch. By using the state legislatures as many different channels through which the voters populated the Senate, the Constitution's original design dispersed the process of selecting Senators over the whole extent of the republic, state by state. In addition, making the selection process for the two chambers separate in this way put their independence of each other on a firm electoral foundation, preventing the concentration of federal legislative power that would have resulted from the Virginia Plan.

The Constitution's original system, by comparison with the Virginia Plan, also enhanced the power of the voters. By putting the voters again at the source of the process of selecting Senators, voters in effect got a second federal vote by means of their vote for their state legislators. Finally, there can be little doubt that the most important benefit of the original system

it worked to preserve the political independence of
dual states.

That was the electoral system for Congress America once had.
The direct election of U.S. senators, the system we have today,
bypasses the state legislatures. The consequences have been many
and profound. Probably the most obvious has been the inevitable
erosion of the independence of the states and of their ability to
counter-balance federal power. The Senate had been a barrier to
the passage of federal laws infringing on the powers reserved to
state governments, but the Senate has abandoned that responsibility under the incentives of the new system of election. Because
the states no longer have a powerful standing body representing
their interests within the federal government, the power of the
federal government has rapidly grown at the expense of the states.
The states increasingly are relegated to functioning as administrative units of today's gargantuan federal government. The Tenth
Amendment has become in our time a dead letter:

> "The powers not delegated to the United States by the Consti-
> tution, nor prohibited by it to the States, are reserved to the
> States respectively, or to the people."

Instead of retaining many of their powers and responsibilities,
and only surrendering a limited number of their powers to the
federal government, as the Framers intended, the states are more
and more entangled in administering federal programs and in
carrying out federal mandates. These mandates are often not
even funded by the federal government; the costs of unfunded
mandates fall on the states. The many new departments of the
federal government which have accumulated in Washington, D.C.

during the Progressive Era, such as HUD (Housing and Urban Development) and HHS (Health and Human Services), involve themselves in, and even direct, functions which the Constitution, as drafted by the Founders, left to the states or to the people.

Today, there are armies of federal bureaucrats who spend their work days writing new regulations and coming up with the penalties which give those regulations the force of law. Their job is determining what you and I cannot do and what we must do. This vast administrative state does not conform to the Founders' vision for the federal government; it exists in complete and perfect violation of Article I, Section 1 of the Constitution:

> "All legislative Powers herein granted shall be vested in a Congress of the United States, which shall consist of a Senate and House of Representatives."

My friend Michael Uhlmann wrote a brilliant review of the book *Is Administrative Law Unlawful?* It appeared in the *Claremont Review of Books* under the title "Appointed Tyrants":

> "Whereas the Constitution celebrated and took elaborate pains to establish government at once limited in scope and republican in form, the overwhelming majority of the laws that now govern the nation consist of administrative edicts promulgated by officials who evince little interest in limited government and are neither chosen by, nor easily controlled by, their fellow citizens."

Determining precisely how many federal regulations enforceable by criminal punishment at the discretion of an administrative agency there are presents great difficulties. According to Douglas Husak of Rutgers in his book *Overcriminalization*, there may be more than 300,000.

In earlier days, during peacetime the ordinary American citizen's direct dealings with the federal government were generally limited to the Post Office. The federal government mainly dealt with issues involving states; in a general sense it dealt with American state governments and with foreign states. For the most part, American citizens' direct dealings with government were largely limited to state and local government—and if you didn't like what they were doing you were always free to move to a new locality or a different state. According to the Founders' vision, our politics was to be vibrantly local and limited in scope. Our contemporary obsession with national politics, the natural result of the centralization of enormous political power in Washington, was not what they intended.

The Ninth and the Tenth Amendments, the final two of the Bill of Rights, are best considered as a complementary pair, each reinforcing the other. Together they make clear the Founders' intent. The Ninth says our rights *are not limited* to the enumerated rights. The Tenth says the powers of the federal government *are limited* to the enumerated powers. Here is the vision of the Founding stated in less than fifty words; a federal government of strictly limited powers, a people guaranteed vast liberty and consequently unbounded opportunity.

It makes sense to consider the Ninth and the Tenth to be the final acts of the Founding and, at the same time, a summary statement of the Founders' work. The Founder's great commission was fulfilled in the Constitution. Jefferson's opening claim, beginning with "We hold these truths to be self-evident", was just over fifty words in length. Isn't it clear that Madison's closing statement of nearly fifty words deserves to be as revered and remembered as Jefferson's opening one?

M adison and the other Founders put much emphasis on the importance of the independence of the states to the preservation of Americans' liberty. Lord Acton, who greatly admired the genius of the Founders, agreed with them:

> "Federalism: It is coordination instead of subordination; association instead of hierarchical order; independent forces curbing each other; balance, therefore, liberty."

We need to remember that when Acton wrote those words American federalism was much more robust than it is now. Direct election of U.S. senators undermined this critically important protection of liberty. The erosion of Americans' individual liberty that has resulted is no doubt the most important consequence of the change.

The Founders would certainly have opposed this change to the Constitution because they would have understood that it would throw the system they had crafted completely out of balance, as it in fact has done.

The Constitutional Amendment which provided for the direct election of senators (the Seventeenth) was ratified in 1913. Earlier that same year the Sixteenth Amendment provided for the progressive income tax. This burst of amendments to the Constitution marks the effective beginning of the Progressive Era in American politics. Changing the federal government's revenue base from tariffs, which are largely self-limiting, removed a fundamental limit to the growth of federal power. By reducing the states politically and providing the federal government with the means to fund virtually unlimited growth, the progressives succeeded in replacing the limited federal government of the Founders with the constantly expanding federal government we have today.

The Eighteenth Amendment, the Prohibition amendment, quickly followed in 1919, at about the crest of the initial wave of progressivism. Americans soon realized that Prohibition was a mistake, and the Eighteenth Amendment was soon repealed. In contrast, the connection between the enormous increase of federal power that has resulted from the Sixteenth and the Seventeenth Amendments has not been as easy for American voters alarmed about increasing federal power to discern.

O ne more point regarding elections: the framers of the Constitution also modified Madison's Virginia Plan for electing the President. Instead of having the two branches of Congress together choose the President, once again the voters initiated the process at the state and local level by choosing the Presidential Electors. The model for this system was the slates of delegates which had represented the people of the individual states at the Constitutional Convention. Leading citizens were to be chosen by the voters for the special purpose of selecting the President. The Electors would assemble in the state in which they were selected, deliberate, and then cast the votes allotted to that state.

Though it does not function as the Founders originally intended, the Electoral College remains an essential Constitutional safeguard of American liberty. As you know, each state is allotted as many electoral votes as it has Senators and members of the House of Representatives. To become President of the United States of America one must even today win the national election state by state. Eliminating the Electoral College and electing the President by the popular vote, as the progressives are determined to do, would transform the office. Its occupant would in effect become the President of the Big Cities of America, and the last vestiges of autonomy guaranteed the individual states by the Constitution's electoral system would be swept away.

The authors of *The Federalist Papers* put great emphasis on the importance of the power of the individual states as a counter-balance to federal power, and on the many benefits of the Constitution's system for electing the Senate and the President. This can cause us some confusion when we open a copy of *The Federalist Papers* and begin to read it for the first time. We need to realize that in these passages, and in others as well, the authors are discussing a Constitutional order we no longer have.

FIVE

The Federalist Papers

"[T]he best commentary on the principles of government, which ever was written."

—THOMAS JEFFERSON

ADAM SMITH'S THIRD MASTERPIECE

"Adam Smith's insight was that we human beings not only pursue our self-interest but seek the approbation of others, and the combination makes freedom work."

—CHARLES MURRAY

Adam Smith's first masterpiece was *The Theory of Moral Sentiments*. In it Smith presented his version of the theory of human nature according to the Scottish Enlightenment: man the social and moral being. Smith grounded social behavior and ethics in the human capacity for sympathy with others:

> "Nature, when she formed man for society, endowed him with an original desire to please, and an original aversion to offend his brethren. She taught him to feel pleasure in their favourable, and pain in their unfavourable regard."

Smith was at the time Professor of Moral Philosophy at the University of Glasgow, but that is not the reason this book on moral philosophy was his first book. For the Scottish thinkers of the era, moral philosophy was fundamental, and Smith always thought of himself primarily as a moral philosopher.

The second masterpiece was *The Wealth of Nations*, the foundational work of modern economics. Defining wealth as economic productivity, not gold or silver, and sounding a note that seems to describe with perfect accuracy our current American circumstance, he wrote:

> "[T]he natural effort of every individual to better his own condition . . . is so powerful a principle, that it is alone, and

without any assistance, not only capable of carrying on the society to wealth and prosperity, but of surmounting a hundred impertinent obstructions with which the folly of human laws too often incumbers its operations."

Smith reconciled this natural inclination of every human to improve his own condition with the moral sentiments by showing how markets enable humans to satisfy themselves by first satisfying another, thereby creating mutually beneficial exchanges. Here is the well-known quotation, presented in full (and not truncated as it often is):

> "But man has almost constant occasion for the help of his brethren, and it is in vain for him to expect it from their benevolence only. He will be more likely to prevail if he can interest their self-love in his favour, and shew them that it is for their own advantage to do for him what he requires of them. Whoever offers to another a bargain of any kind, proposes to do this. *Give me that which I want, and you shall have this which you want, is the meaning of every such offer; and it is in this manner that we obtain from one another the far greater part of those good offices which we stand in need of* [Emphasis added]. It is not from the benevolence of the butcher, the brewer, or the baker, that we expect our dinner, but from their regard to their own interest. We address ourselves, not to their humanity but to their self-love, and never talk to them of our own necessities but of their advantages."

Smith planned to produce, and often referred to, a third major work, a book on political theory. The third book was long delayed and finally never published. At Smith's insistence, his manuscript notes for the book were burned when he died.

The non-existence of the book on political theory has been minutely examined by Smith scholars. We know that Smith's position as tutor to the young Duke of Buccleuch had provided him with more time for philosophical work than his teaching load and administrative responsibilities at Glasgow had allowed, enabling him to finish *The Wealth of Nations* in 1776. The scholarly consensus is that Smith's decision to turn down a subsequent offer to be tutor to the young Duke of Hamilton was a tragic error. Smith instead accepted an appointment to the Scottish Commissionership of Customs in 1778. The demands of the office together with Smith's characteristic conscientiousness left him little time for philosophy. The final act, the burning of his notes, has served to heighten the sense of loss associated with the missing third book.

However, we can, with Charles Murray, safely assume that the book would have extended the arguments of *Sentiments* and *Wealth*, applying the same principles noted above to the theory of political liberty.

Although we do not have Smith's book, we do have a masterpiece from exactly that time which very precisely fits the pattern suggested by Murray. I am of course referring to *The Federalist Papers,* the brainchild of Alexander Hamilton, with much help from James Madison and, to a lesser extent, John Jay. The timing is certainly right. *Sentiments* was published in 1759, *Wealth,* in 1776, and *The Federalist Papers*, in 1788, just in time to fit into Smith's life and work; Smith died in 1790.

To suggest, as I am, that we have in *The Federalist Papers* a worthy fulfillment of Smith's promised third book by three Americans working in Smith's tradition may not actually be that far-fetched. Of course, we know that the Founders were steeped in the Scottish Enlightenment tradition, and that the American Enlightenment was deeply rooted in the Scottish one. However, this was in some respects a two-way relationship, especially for Adam Smith. Smith's biographer, Nicholas Phillipson, points out that America's example was of critical significance for Smith in the development of his thinking in his best known work:

> "In *The Wealth of Nations* America was to provide him with the most striking and decisive illustration of the possibilities of the civilizing process in a part of the civilized world that had never been encumbered by feudal laws and institutions, and whose distance from Europe had ensured that the principles of natural liberty had already guided some aspects of its economic development."

The index to *The Wealth of Nations* contains more than a hundred entries under "America."

Economists commonly give Adam Smith enormous and much deserved credit for envisioning our modern world although he lived during a time in which his native Scotland offered barely a glimpse of our world. But, as Phillipson writes, America had provided Smith "with the most striking and decisive illustration of the possibilities" offered by "the principles of natural liberty" which were already at work in America, in economics and in American life in general. The economic system and the principles of natural liberty in the process of being realized in America, that civilization of ours which has done so much to create the modern world, were already clear enough during the era of the Founding to be discerned by the genius of Adam Smith.

During the last years of Smith's life, while he was chafing under the demands of his post as Commissioner of Customs and lamenting its demands on his time, the Americans were conducting experiments in political liberty, and, while learning from what worked and what did not work, simultaneously engaged among themselves in a kind of ongoing seminar in the theory of political liberty, all the while working under the pressure of needing to come up with a system of government to replace the Colonial one.

If Smith had been free to focus his time and energy on the third book, we can safely assume he would have followed closely the fast-paced learning process of the Founders, and that what he learned from the Founders would have greatly influenced that book. It is likely that the Americans' influence would have even been greater than it was on *The Wealth of Nations* itself.

Provided with a society unencumbered by a feudal past with which to experiment, placed by a unique historical circumstance in positions of political leadership that made it possible for them to conduct their experiments, and fully equipped with the innovations of the Scottish Enlightenment, the authors of *The Federalist Papers* were uniquely positioned to carry Adam Smith's great project to a successful conclusion, and as Jefferson wrote, create the best commentary on the principles of government ever written.

MADISON'S FAMOUS ARGUMENT— THE EXTENDED REPUBLIC

"The smaller the society, the fewer probably will be the distinct parties and interests composing it, . . . the more easily will they concert and execute their plans of oppression . . . Extend

*the sphere, and you take in a greater variety of parties and
interests; you make it less probable that a majority of the whole
will . . . invade the rights of other citizens."*
—JAMES MADISON, *FEDERALIST 10*

Federalist 10 is often cited as the single most important statement of American political thought, and the passage above presents, very briefly, Madison's most famous argument in No. 10.

Stated briefly, Madison's argument is this: a multiplicity of factions in an extended republic makes each faction less dangerous
than it would be in a small society. An extended republic of the
kind the Founders envisioned, Madison argues, has this built-in
feature that is a safeguard of the rights of its citizens that arises
from the very nature of the society itself.

This argument and *Federalist 10* have generated a mountain
of scholarly writings over the course of the past century. Scholars
have for the most part heatedly disputed how they are to be
understood. Instead of delving into the twists and turns of all of
these controversies, let's find out for ourselves if we can make
sense of this argument.

Just as we found we needed to touch bases with Thomas Reid
and Francis Hutcheson to understand the Declaration of Independence, a bit of help from Adam Smith and Thomas Reid will
enable us to avoid the tangles and confusions that have marred
a century of *Federalist 10* scholarship.

We need to begin by noting that, although Madison's famous
argument addresses the nature of *society* in an extended republic,
Madison's overall subject in No. 10 is the Constitution's design for
the *government*. Since the argument has been the source of so
much scholarly confusion and dispute, let us begin by examining

it. Once that is done, we will be ready to turn to what Madison has to say in No. 10 about government.

Despite the extraordinary volume of scholarship focused on this argument, its roots in the Scottish Enlightenment have gone largely unnoticed. In a brilliant exception to this trend, Samuel Fleischacker points out that Madison's argument is taken directly from Adam Smith. In his brilliant paper "Scottish Philosophy and the American Founding" he makes the case that Madison's argument is an extension of the argument Smith offers in *The Wealth of Nations* for the advantages of a multiplicity of religious sects.

In *Wealth*, Smith argues that a multiplicity of sects makes it difficult for any single religious group to become large enough to threaten the whole society. As Professor Fleischacker observes: "Smith's analysis of what happens to religious sects when left alone by government follows . . . the logic of the market: competition . . . [benefits] society. And just this logic underlies Madison's analysis of factions." For Smith and for Madison, in faith as in economics, their answers have the same logic: freedom of religion and the free market, instead of a religious establishment and a royal sovereign doling out economic privileges to royal favorites. So too, says Madison, for how society, and as we shall see, government, will function in an extended republic.

Madison returns to this argument, and again ties it to Smith's example of the multiplicity of religious sects, in *Federalist 51*. In the extended republic,

"the society itself will be broken into so many parts, interests and classes of citizens, that the rights of individuals or of the minority, will be in little danger from interested [biased; as

opposed to impartial or disinterested. Today, still following
Madison, we speak of 'special interests'] combinations of the
majority. In a free government, the security for civil rights must
be the same as for religious rights. It consists in the multiplicity
of interests, and in the other, in the multiplicity of sects."

Scholars have managed to come up with a truly dazzling array of
ways of failing to make sense of this argument. Their difficulties
and the resulting scholarly controversies are the direct result of
the scholarly consensus that overlooks the American Enlightenment and its roots in the Scottish Enlightenment.

Madison's argument is actually quite straightforward. Here is
the central claim: a small republic can offer no solution to the
problem of a majority faction oppressing the minority. Think
of it in this way: we can imagine the elected government of a
republic of Manhattan Island with today's population outlawing
the ownership of automobiles by private citizens and rescinding
the tax-exempt status of churches. But "extend the sphere" of the
republic to include voters who live in rural Texas and in Bible Belt
states, and assembling a like-minded national majority in support
of those policies becomes a much more difficult challenge.

The important point for us to grasp is that Madison's argument
for how society will function in a free republic follows the logic of
Adam Smith's analysis of how the free market functions. And just
as it is the case, as Smith demonstrated in *The Wealth of Nations*,
that the more we extend the market the better it serves our needs,
Madison argues the more we extend the republic the better it
secures our rights. Madison's extended republic and Smith's
extended market order function in the same way. We rely on our
fellow citizens, and on the variety of their interests in competition

and cooperation with our own, to secure our economic needs and to conduct our social lives. In the same way, because ours is an extended republic, the variety of the interests and concerns of our fellow citizens can help protect our rights.

Given the difficulties scholars have found in understanding Madison's argument, it is remarkable that they have been in agreement about its significance. On this one point, certainly, they have been correct. Madison's argument is a magnificent illustration of how the Founders made use of the intellectual materials provided them by the Scots.

According to the Scots, because we are social beings endowed with a moral sense, human society simply is a continual series of voluntary exchanges among its members. Here is Adam Smith on this idea, considered from the viewpoint of economics:

> "This division of labour, from which so many advantages are derived, is not originally the effect of any human wisdom, which foresees and intends that general opulence to which it gives occasion. It is the necessary, though very slow and gradual, consequence of a certain propensity in human nature which has in view no such extensive utility; the propensity to truck, barter, and exchange one thing for another."

Smith is saying that our natural inclination to exchange one thing for another is the original source of the prosperity civilization provides. The propensity to "truck, barter, and exchange" gives rise to the division of labor which is the source of the wealth of nations.

But the larger point is that economic exchanges are only a fraction, only one aspect, of that unending process of exchanges, perpetually renewed, which constitutes social living. By shaking

hands in greeting and by shaking hands when we make an agreement, by serving our customers or clients well and by putting in
a good word for a person who has served us well, and in a myriad
of other similar actions from keeping appointments to looking
out for our neighbors, we carry on the life of society. The Scots
recognized the moral perfection, as well as the material benefits,
of achieving our ends by dealing with others as beings of equal
dignity, as free co-participants in the life of society. As social
beings endowed with moral sense we realize ourselves in shared
and open participation with our neighbors. Madison shows us how
the Founders applied that new understanding of human society
to an even newer understanding of politics.

Here is Thomas Sowell in his book *On Classical Economics* on
the political and social implications of the radically new paradigm
that guided Madison's thinking:

> "The idea of a spontaneously self-equilibrating system—the
> market economy— . . . made part of the tradition of classical
> economics by Adam Smith, represented a radical departure, not
> only in analysis of causation but also in seeing a reduced role for
> political, intellectual, or other leaders as guides or controllers
> of the masses. Even today, many have not yet grasped the full
> implications of self-equilibrating interactions . . ."

The fact that many have not yet been able to grasp the full social
and political implications of spontaneously self-equilibrating systems means the thinking of the Founders was, and still is today,
very advanced indeed.

The spontaneous collaboration of free citizens in the Founders'
extended republic is what made America flourish. It turned out

that the new system envisioned by the Founders did not merely bestow the blessings of liberty, as it was intended to do; it also worked better than every system that had gone before. It certainly worked better economically. As the economist Deirdre McCloskey wrote in her brilliant book *Bourgeois Dignity*:

> "Give people liberty to work and to invent and to invest, and treat them with dignity, and you get fast [economic growth]."

The successful example of America's open, innovative society changed the world, challenging every other system and inspiring people everywhere.

And thanks to the brilliant analysis of F. A. Hayek and others we now even have an explanation of why Madison's extended republic functions so well. The foundation of America's success has been shown to be the nature of human knowledge. The Founders' republic works so well because of the most fundamental fact about human knowledge; human knowledge, and especially the knowledge that matters most to our daily lives, is *dispersed*; it exists among the minds of all humanity. The baker does not have to master the craft of brewing, and the brewer and the baker can both rely on the plumber, and so on *ad infinitum*. No single person knows, no single person can know, even the tiniest fraction of human knowledge. America's extended republic, like the extended market order itself, works by bringing that dispersed human knowledge together in order to solve, with astonishing efficiency compared to every other system, the problems of daily existence.

By bringing together Smith's vision of a free market and the Founders' vision of a social order and a system of government befitting a free people, the American republic provided its citizens with liberty and opportunity far beyond anything human beings had ever known before.

B ecause scholars who emphasize the influence of Locke on the Founders also tend to emphasize the importance of Montesquieu to the Founding, we should briefly note that Madison's argument for the benefits of an extended republic turned Montesquieu on his head. The Baron de Montesquieu, a French aristocrat and follower of Locke, was the French thinker of the Enlightenment era who the Americans found to be most useful. As usual, the Founders took from Montesquieu only what they found useful, particularly his analysis of the British system's separation of legislative and executive powers. The separation of political power, Montesquieu argued, provided a mechanism for self-correction within the government, just as the body's self-correcting mechanisms work to maintain health.

But according to Montesquieu in *The Spirit of the Laws* a republic must be small if it is to survive. He argued that "an extensive republic" could not long endure:

> "It is natural for a republic to have only a small territory;
> otherwise it cannot long subsist . . . It was the spirit of the
> Greek republics to be as contented with their territories as
> with their laws."

Madison did not follow Montesquieu on this doctrine, although it was a fundamental one according to Montesquieu. The important point for our purpose is that Madison came to a completely different vision of what is possible for an extended republic, one that is in alignment with the thinking of Adam Smith.

In addition, Montesquieu, like Edmund Burke, argued that society and government require a very large role for an aristocracy in order to have stability. Madison displayed perfect independence of Montesquieu on that doctrine also.

That the success of the Founders' extended republic is based on its alignment with the nature of human knowledge reveals the brilliance of the Founders. We have seen that their systematic analysis of political liberty was deeply rooted in a philosophical examination of human understanding. That examination encompassed human understanding of human nature and of nature by way of moral sense philosophy and the philosophy of common sense realism. History has shown that the Founders' design did succeed, so today we know that what they built has demonstrated that it has what it takes to stand the test of time.

There is no doubt that many, perhaps even all, of those who today reject the vision of the Founders do so because of their failure to understand the new paradigm that made the modern world. They live in the modern world without understanding how it came to be. Their thinking is stuck in the ancient mold according to which the economy and society need a ruler vested with sovereign power to provide direction.

Under top-down systems, mankind has lived with economic stagnation and political repression. Top-down systems, economic stagnation, and political repression go together, as history, from pre-Revolutionary France to today's North Korea, endlessly repeats; the more the system is top-down, the greater the resulting economic stagnation and the greater the political repression.

The Founders' focus was liberty. Their design provided a limited role for government and a maximum role for spontaneously self-equilibrating systems in American society and in the American economy; they designed the federal government to fit into their vision of American society. Here is Thomas Jefferson in his first inaugural address:

> "Still one thing more, fellow-citizens—a wise and frugal Government, which shall restrain men from injuring one another, shall leave them otherwise free to regulate their own pursuits of industry and improvement, and shall not take from the mouth of labor the bread it has earned. This is the sum of good government . . ."

Those who today do not share the Founders' vision for society naturally reject the Founders' vision of government.

MADISON'S FAMOUS ARGUMENT, PART 2—REPRESENTATION

"No man is allowed to be a judge in his own cause, because his interest would certainly bias his judgment."
—JAMES MADISON, *FEDERALIST 10*

This self-evident proposition is the key to understanding Madison's whole theory of representative government.

It is as fundamental to the Constitution as the self-evident truth that all men are created equal is to the Declaration of Independence. That no man can rightfully be a judge in his own cause is the explanation for the lengths to which the Framers went to divide and disperse the political power of the elected officials of the federal government.

The Constitution has the design it has so that we can have self-government without being judges in our own cause. Because the monarch is a judge in his own cause, monarchy violates this self-evident truth. But to make the people a judge in their own cause violates it equally. A direct democracy, one in which the people, in Madison's words in No. 10, "assemble and administer the government in person," makes the people judges in their own cause. Direct democracy therefore also fails to meet the standard of a government of laws and not of men.

To understand Madison's thinking, consider how a judge functions. If you get into a legal dispute, the result is likely to be that you and your adversary will eventually appear before a judge. The judge has the responsibility to make a disinterested, unbiased judgment based on the law and the facts of the case. Delegating the tasks of governing to individuals chosen by the citizens is like delegating the tasks of judging to individuals also chosen, directly or indirectly, by the citizens. The representative and constitutional republic meets the "judging in one's own cause" test. It puts governing at one remove from the people, making possible a government of law and not of men. Just as the judge is bound by the law, the Congress in making law, the President in executing the laws, and the Supreme Court in adjudicating the law are bound by the Constitution. In Jefferson's words quoted above, "bind [them] down from mischief by the chains of the Constitution."

The self-evident truth that no man can be a judge in his own cause leads us, as it did the Founders, by inexorable logic to the representative and constitutional republic as the only choice for the government of a free people.

"We the people . . . "

We can understand the Founders better by considering a contrast with the English. As the result of the Glorious Revolution, their monarch no longer has unlimited royal sovereignty by divine right. However, legal power in Great Britain is still vested in a sovereign—now the Queen (or King) in Parliament. The English are not citizens; they are royal subjects. The phrase "La Reyne le veult" signifies this fact. Those words are Norman French (a residue of the conquest of England by the Normans under William the Conqueror in 1066) for "The Queen wills it." The phrase signifies royal assent to a bill passed by Parliament.

Here is my friend Hadley Arkes in his brilliant essay "Building Democracy" on the critical difference between English and American law:

> "In Chisholm v. Georgia (1793), the first case to elicit a set of opinions in the new Supreme Court, James Wilson remarked that the law in America would stand on a different foundation from that of the law in England. The latter began with a sovereign issuing commands. But in America, said Wilson, 'the sovereign, when traced to its source, must be found in the man' [Emphasis in the original]. It is to be found, that is, in a natural person, tendering his consent to the terms on which he is governed."

Chief Justice John Jay made the same point in *Chisholm*, writing of the "great and glorious principle, that the people are the sovereign of this country."

"The Queen wills it" is a far cry from "We the people." According to the Founders' vision, we are to manage our own lives as free and sovereign citizens, living under laws which take the form of general rules applied equally to every citizen and which are enacted by our elected representatives, linked by social and commercial ties spontaneously generated amongst ourselves, and allied politically with our like-minded fellow citizens.

Professor Arkes continues in his essay by quoting Allan Greenberg making the observation that "in the United States, this new democratic republic, the rights and prerogatives that were once reserved for . . . the kings of Europe now belong to every citizen." In America, we citizens are the sovereign, and the rights and responsibilities of sovereignty are ours.

We the people exercise our sovereignty in two ways. First, and most fundamentally, we did so originally by ratifying the Constitution. "We the people" are the first three words in the Constitution:

> "We the people of the United States . . . do ordain and establish this Constitution for the United States of America."

The Founding generation ratified the Constitution and bequeathed to each succeeding generation the responsibility of preserving it. Preserving the Constitution is the sovereign citizen's primary responsibility. As Madison wrote in *Federalist 53*:

> "The important distinction so well understood in America between a constitution established by the people, and unalterable by the government, seems to have been little understood and less observed in any other country."

"Established by the people, and unalterable by the government." Tragically, this important distinction and the citizen's responsibility it entails, once so well understood in America, have been obscured by the progressive doctrine of "the living Constitution." According to that doctrine, the Constitution is alterable by the government and the Supreme Court, according to the latest ideas and the politics of the moment. Consequently, the Founders would certainly say we now live in an increasingly post-Constitutional America, and they would fault us for failing in our most fundamental responsibility of sovereignty.

Second, in each election we exercise our sovereignty by selecting, for strictly limited periods of service, fellow citizens to conduct the work of government for us. As Professor Randy Barnett wrote in his book *Restoring the Lost Constitution*,

> "the appropriate legal construct is not the surrender of rights to a master, but the delegation of powers to an agent. As [Chief Justice John] Marshall himself wrote: 'It is the plain dictate of common sense, and the whole political system is founded on the idea, that the departments of government are the agents of the nation . . .' When a principal engages an agent, the agent can be empowered to act on behalf of and subject to the control of the principal, while at the same time the principal retains all his rights."

In the American idea, in the vision of the Founders, we never surrender our sovereignty. But bit by bit we have been surrendering it. We have been doing that by electing to office people who are indifferent to the Constitution, or hostile to it, or ignorant of it.

Because the responsibilities of sovereignty are ours, the success of the American Republic and the preservation of the Constitution ultimately depend on you and me. Here we reach the bedrock of the republic the Founders designed for us. The Founders' design ultimately relies on our shared capacity for moral and common sense thinking, that endowment of our human nature so carefully explored and analyzed by Hutcheson, Smith, and Reid. Madison put it this way in *Federalist 55*:

> "As there is a degree of depravity in mankind which requires a certain degree of circumspection and distrust, so there are other qualities in human nature which justify a certain portion of esteem and confidence. Republican government presupposes the existence of these qualities in a higher degree than any other form."

A nd scale does matter to a representative republic, though in a totally different way than Montesquieu believed. The republican form of government can be representative in two distinct ways. In the first and most fundamental way, Madison proposed the direct election of members of the House, and that is the way it was in the original Constitution, and still today. The members of the House are to represent the local area in the federal legislature, and they are subject to being replaced in the next election if the voters are not satisfied with their service.

The second sense of representation deserves a closer look. As we have seen, the Constitution provided for the state legislatures to choose the U.S. senators for each state. In that case, the state legislators, chosen by the voters, again act as the voters' representatives, this time in selecting the senators. The Founders believed that was a better way than direct election for this office. Obviously the Framers were not opposed to direct election on principle since that is the method they chose for the House, so we must ask why they chose indirect election for the Senate.

The Founders believed it is the better way for the simplest of reasons. Just as the members of the House will naturally be champions for the local issues of concern to their neighbors in their individual districts, the U.S. senators are to be the champions for state issues, for their states' governments, and for the people of their states in general. Clearly, the members of the state legislatures are well positioned to select the persons capable of championing their state's concerns in the federal legislature.

We no longer think this way about U.S. senators but perhaps it is worth a brief discussion.

Today, we elect members of the House and the Senate in the same way, though there are significant differences in their responsibilities. The way we fill those offices no longer reflects those differences. In addition, except for the least populous states, there is also this very great difference: your congressperson is your neighbor, at least by comparison with your senator. My congressman's district office is nearby, and I have gotten into conversation with him at a restaurant we both frequent and at the dealership where it happens we both take our cars for repairs. I have known the owner of the restaurant for many years, and he happens to be a good friend of our congressman. This may be different from your experience, but I believe the principle is clear. We are in a good position to make an informed vote, and we can at least in principle more easily have good information, when we are voting on the most local level, either for our U.S. congressperson or for our state legislators.

In the same way, the leading citizens of the state, the people most likely to be capable of representing the state in the federal government are, in a manner of speaking, local to the members of the legislature; they are part, as it were, of the legislators' locale. The legislators are part of the "neighborhood" of state leaders, and are thereby positioned to make an informed choice about which leader could do the best job representing the state in the federal government. In addition, by virtue of the problems they deal with in the legislature, the state legislators are likely to be better informed than the typical voter about the issues confronting the state government, especially issues between their state and the federal government.

The Founders thought this system was necessary to preserve the independence of the states. A case can also be made that it provided a good chance of getting able people into the Senate. Consider this example: I am thinking of an actual recent U.S. senator. He was re-elected to the Senate repeatedly. His colleagues were inescapably aware that he was no more capable of making sense when he talked than he was capable of stopping himself once he got started. He was notorious for bringing Senate hearings to a standstill. Blessed with a staff that did an outstanding job of providing cover for him, a friendly press in his home state that is allied with his political party, he represented a one-party state. The voters of his state somehow seemed never to realize the problem.

Isn't it clear from this example that state legislators would be in a very good position to make a sound judgment about which of their number had the capacity to represent their state's interests effectively in the Senate?

Of course, this same logic applies to the Constitution's original design for electing the President. The voters would select the presidential Electors from among the political leaders they knew well. The Electors would then be charged with the very great responsibility of representing their voters in making the choice for the office in which character and wisdom most matter in the American system.

So here in the Senate and in the presidential Electors we have the logic of Madison's second sense of representation: although increasing the extent of the *society* makes it more difficult for a majority to oppress a minority, increasing the extent of the *electoral territory* to too great an extent makes it more difficult for the voter to make an informed choice. If we can detect faint echoes of Montesquieu's doctrine regarding the extensive republic here, then it is his doctrine utterly transformed and reconceived in the service of a vision for government unlike anything the world had seen before.

O f course, the soundness of the whole system depends on the voters making good choices in the first place. James Wilson wrote this about the Constitution in 1788:

> "If the people, at their elections, take care to choose none but representatives that are wise and good, their representatives will take care, in their turn, to choose or appoint none but such as are wise and good also."

The sovereign people need to choose wisely, just as royal sovereigns need to choose wisely the people they select to conduct the business of governing. In either case, the failure of the administration chosen by the sovereign is not the end of the sovereign. There is always the option of a new administration—unless the administration's failure leads to a military defeat or an economic or social collapse that wrests the government away from the sovereign.

⚜

MADISON'S FAMOUS ARGUMENT, PART 3— THE LOGIC OF THE MARKET, EXTENDED

"No man is allowed to be a judge in his own cause, because his interest would certainly bias his judgment . . . And what are the different classes of legislators but advocates and parties to the causes which they determine? . . . Yet the parties are, and must be, themselves the judges; and the most numerous party, or, in other words, the most powerful faction must be expected to prevail . . . The inference to which we are brought is, that the causes of faction cannot be removed [from government], and that relief is only to be sought in the means of controlling its effects"
—JAMES MADISON, FEDERALIST 10

We earlier considered this argument for what it reveals about Madison's reliance on Thomas Reid's philosophical *method*. Let us now turn to the *content* of his argument.

Here Madison addresses the problem of faction *within* the government.

The American people choose their representatives to act as their agents. Consequently, a republic will necessarily reflect the society at large; the society of an extended republic will have a multiplicity of factions. Its government will therefore also have a multiplicity of factions.

Although, as we have seen, a multiplicity of factions in an extended society provides its own barriers to one faction invading the rights of the minority, it cannot prevent a sufficiently numerous party in society prevailing overwhelmingly at the ballot box. How can such a political majority, once achieved, be prevented from using the government to oppress a minority? Since, as Madison says, we cannot eliminate that possibility, by what means, he asks, can we so design government itself to provide additional protection of the rights of individuals and of the minority from being violated by the politicians put in power by a powerful majority?

Samuel Fleischacker's analysis again points the way to the logic of the market; competition benefits society. Madison's brilliant answer is that competition *within* government can also benefit society. By dispersing federal power among the different branches of government, the design of government introduces the possibility of competition within the government.

Madison returns to this issue in *Federalist 51*. A look at No. 51 will help us understand No. 10. Here is the argument in No. 51 as explained by Arthur Herman in his magnificent book, *The Cave and the Light*:

> "In Madison's vision, the legislative, executive, and judicial branches of government would have their powers separated out, so that instead of cooperating they would be locked in permanent but dynamic competition. No group of cunning and unscrupulous men could seize control of one branch to dominate the others . . . because other groups of cunning and unscrupulous men would naturally use the other branches to fight back . . . 'ambition must be made to counteract ambition,' Madison wrote. In this way, 'through supplying opposite and rival interests,' the separation of powers in the federal Constitution would 'supply the defect [lack] of better motives.'"

What Madison did here was truly remarkable. He advanced a radically new vision for government. That vision took its direction from Adam Smith's analysis of how a free market works. Compare the logic of Madison's vision for the government with the logic of this famous passage from Smith's *The Wealth of Nations*:

> "It is not from the benevolence of the butcher, the brewer, or the baker, that we expect our dinner, but from their regard to their own interest."

Smith showed that a system that allows for the free play of rival interests in commerce benefits the individual and benefits society in general. Those benefits flow from such a system as if the rivals had "better motives" than simply their own interest. Madison extends Smith's demonstration to argue that just as the rival interests of brewers and bakers operating in a free market provide us with competitive prices and competition in quality to our benefit, the rival interests of politicians operating in the defined arena of limited government can provide protection for our liberties. The politicians' rivalry can make it, in Madison's words, "less probable that a majority of the whole will . . . invade the rights of other citizens."

In fact, if we take a closer look at that section of No. 51 Herman quotes above, it is clear that for Madison the principle of the benefits of competing interests illuminates "the whole system of human affairs."

> "The policy of supplying, by opposite and rival interests, the defect [lack] of better motives, might be traced through the whole system of human affairs, private as well as public."

Adam Smith's account of the free market and Madison's account of the American system of liberty have a common baseline. Smith showed that in a free market rivalry improves economic performance, benefiting everyone. Smith and Madison's larger point is that competing interests make for improved performance in general. The competing interests of rivals are the heart and soul of improved performance across the range of human activities, from the Olympic Games and the National Football League to the rapid technological innovation that characterizes our society.

Madison put that understanding to work in explaining the Framers' design of the American system of self-government. We know today that free markets promote prosperity by providing for the interplay of rival interests. Madison's point is that a political system that is properly designed to allow for the interplay of rival political interests can promote liberty. Where there is unified political power, as in an absolute monarchy, or in Revolutionary France, or in Mao's China, the people have no safety from their government. Consequently, governmental power must be dispersed, instead of concentrated, if liberty is to be preserved.

If Madison's account of the rivalries of political ambition strikes us as much more brutal than Smith's account of the rivalries among brewers or bakers that is only to be expected, the effect of power on human nature being what it is. *Federalist 51*, you may remember, is where we also find this famous quote of Madison we noted earlier:

"If men were angels, no government would be necessary. If angels were to govern men, neither external nor internal controls on government would be necessary."

Your friendly neighborhood brewer may be as eager for your patronage as your senator is for your vote, but the brewer does not have any of the political powers of coercion that the senator has; he only has the opportunity to seek your patronage. Nor is he, in the course of his work as a brewer, likely to be subjected to anything like the enormous temptations that the powers of office bring the senator's way. Today in America a fear of the influence of business interests drives many voters to vote for ever-increasing governmental power. This would seem very strange to the Founders.

Of course, introducing competition within the government can only do so much. Competition within government does not change the fact that government is force and that it is a monopoly. The Founders understood that government power must be limited, as well as dispersed. Because government is force and because government is a monopoly, government is unlike the spontaneous order that arises among individuals and groups interacting freely in society or in voluntary exchanges among people in free markets. That is why government's functions must be strictly defined and its power must be strictly limited. The Constitution strictly defines the powers of government, disperses power within the federal government, reserves certain powers to the individual states, and also places certain rights of the citizen beyond the reach of government. It does all that so that competition within government can, in Madison's words, work to the benefit of society.

Those who today reject the vision of Madison and the Founders seek to turn that vision upside down. They strive for an ever-expanding role for government and a dwindling role for spontaneous order in society. More and more government at every level means less and less is left to the spontaneous order generated by citizens making free choices. According to the Founders, the rightful purpose of limited government is the protection of liberty.

More and more government means the abandonment of the Founders' vision for America's system of government and the abandonment of the kind of society the Founders had in mind when they designed that government.

SIX

Religion and the American Enlightenment

"Far from being rivals or enemies, religion and law are twin sisters, friends, and mutual assistants. Indeed, these two sciences run into each other. The divine law, as discovered by reason and the moral sense, forms an essential part of both."

—JAMES WILSON, LECTURES ON LAW, 1791

RELIGION IN THE AMERICA OF THE ENLIGHTENMENT

"In the America of the Enlightenment . . . the specifically American form of Christianity—undogmatic, moralistic rather than creedal, tolerant but strong, and all-pervasive of society—was born, and . . . the Great Awakening was its midwife."

—PAUL JOHNSON, *A HISTORY OF THE AMERICAN PEOPLE*

The Great Awakening was the great Protestant revival that swept the American colonies before the American Revolution. One of the pivotal events of American history, its importance to America's Founding was enormous yet is often overlooked. Paul Johnson puts it like this:

> "The Great Awakening was thus the proto-revolutionary event, *the formative moment in American history,* preceding the political drive for independence and making it possible. It crossed all religious and sectarian boundaries . . . and turned what had been a series of European-style churches into American ones." [Emphasis added]

It also broke down the geographical boundaries. Each colony had been largely a world unto itself, more oriented to London than to its neighbors. The Great Awakening changed all that. George Whitefield, "the Grand Itinerant," made seven continental tours between 1740 and 1770, speaking to enormous crowds everywhere he went—10,000, an astonishing number in those days, was not uncommon. Whitefield became the first truly American public figure, equally well known in every colony. Whitefield and the other revival preachers of the era brought about a new sense of geographical unity, a new sense of what it meant to be an American, and at the same time gave American Christianity its unique character.

The Great Awakening has had an enduring impact on America. It persisted in the great camp-meetings that played such an important role in American life for the next two hundred years, and it persists in the great non-denominational mega-churches of our day.

Even the founding of Princeton, the *alma mater* of Benjamin Rush and James Madison, and the call for Witherspoon to come to America are the direct result of the Great Awakening. In fact, the Great Awakening prepared the way for the American Revolution in too many ways to be counted. Growing as it did out of a period of deep religious fervor and ferment, the American Revolution was not going to be an anti-religious revolution like the one in France. In the words of John Adams, and extending a passage quoted earlier in the section on the story of Benjamin Rush:

> "The Revolution was effected before the War commenced. The Revolution was in the mind and hearts of the people: and change in their religious sentiments of their duties and obligations."

The Great Awakening and the American Enlightenment together made the Founders' achievement possible.

Lord Acton traced the history of liberty as the story of mankind's struggle down through the centuries to realize the political implications of the Gospel. Harry Jaffa agrees, putting it like this:

> "That the equality of human souls in the sight of God ought to be translated into a political structure of equal political rights

has come to be regarded as the most authentic interpretation of the Gospel itself."

It was the Founders' great achievement, after nearly two millennia, to make equal political rights that authentic interpretation.

America's unique form of Christianity was matched by the uniqueness of the American Enlightenment, and the American combination of the Enlightenment and of Christianity made the American Experiment what it was and is. That combination is perfectly evident from the beginning:

> "We hold these Truths to be self-evident, that all men are cre-
> ated equal, that they are endowed by their Creator with certain
> unalienable Rights . . . "

The Declaration opens with the Enlightenment idea of self-evident truth and the claim that we are *created* equal by our Creator.

EXCEPTIONAL AMERICA

*"There is no country in the world in which the boldest political theo-
ries of the eighteenth-century philosophers are put so effectively
into practice as in America. Only their anti-religious doctrines
have never made any headway in that country."*
—ALEXIS DE TOCQUEVILLE

This remarkable pair of sentences is frequently quoted today by those who attempt to explain America's uniqueness. Tocqueville in a few words gives us a vivid picture of America. Reversing the usual formula, in a few words he depicts what could not be shown with a thousand pictures.

But does this vivid portrait of America tell the real story?

That first sentence certainly points to something important. The Founders had acted on the boldest of political theories, and the boldest theory of all was that the people are sovereign. That theory was perhaps even bolder than bold. In that era wasn't it actually a contradiction in terms? After all, a sovereign was a king or queen; it was the role of the people to be ruled and the role of the sovereign to rule.

The Founders had staked everything on the theory that the people could rule themselves. Looking back from the present we can fail to understand what a radical departure their political experiment was, can fail to appreciate how boldly the Founders gambled on the political theories they had derived from the eighteenth-century philosophers they had studied so closely. We can also fail to appreciate how carefully the Founders proceeded in their political thinking. Putting their bold theories, as Tocqueville wrote, "effectively into practice" was itself a work of collective genius, something even rarer and more precious than great philosophy.

The second sentence correctly points toward America's other way of being unique. It is certainly true that "anti-religious doctrines had never made any headway" in the America Tocqueville visited. He reported that "[Americans] always answered, without a moment's hesitation, that a civilized community, especially one that enjoys the benefit of freedom, cannot exist without religion." The contrast with his native France was stark. Voltaire boasted of his atheism, and he and the other philosophers of the French Enlightenment were fiercely opposed to religion. There was nothing surprising in the fact that the French Revolution resulted in the murder of priests and the confiscation of church property.

However, Tocqueville makes a significant error in the passage quoted at the top of this page. For our purposes, the important point is that this error nearly always escapes notice today. For Tocqueville, quite naturally, "the eighteenth century philosophers" are the Enlightenment philosophers of his native France. That is also the reason his error nearly always goes unnoticed today. Today the French Enlightenment has eclipsed all other developments during the Age of Enlightenment. Consequently, writers today who use the Tocqueville quote share with him the assumption that the French Enlightenment essentially *was* the Enlightenment.

But there was a simple reason Tocqueville found that the anti-religious doctrines of the French Enlightenment had never made any headway in America. The Founders had not relied on the *philosophes* of the French Enlightenment. The Founders relied on an entirely different set of eighteenth century philosophers. Those Enlightenment philosophers and the Founders shared neither the anti-religious views nor the political theories of the French.

John Witherspoon, James Madison's teacher and mentor, can show us quite a lot about the Founders' different perspective. Like Thomas Reid and Francis Hutcheson, Witherspoon, in addition to being a scholar and a professor, was also a Presbyterian minister. He came to America in answer to a call to the missionary field, charged with the responsibility of building up the college established by the Presbyterians for the education of their ministry in and for America. Witherspoon certainly earned the right to be counted as a member in good standing of both the Scottish and the American Enlightenments, and like his colleagues in Scotland

and in America, he was not a foe of religion but instead a deeply religious man and a champion of religious liberty.

Nor, of course, did the Founders subscribe to the political theories of the French Enlightenment. So, the question becomes this: whose political theories did the Founders "put so effectively into practice"?

By now, the answer is I hope clear. To understand the *philosophical* thinking of the Founders, we must look to those philosophers of the eighteenth century they actually relied on—for example, to Thomas Reid, whose philosophy of common sense realism undergirded the Founders' boldest theory of all, the theory that the people are capable of self-government, to Adam Smith, whose analysis of a free market showed that it worked so well because it was largely a self-governing system, and to Francis Hutcheson whose analysis of rights alienable and unalienable guided the thinking of the Founders. But to understand the *political theories* of the American Founders we need to look to the Founders themselves. The bold political theories they so effectively put into practice were their own.

America's Founders, not the French *philosophes*, were the boldest political thinkers of the eighteenth century.

Of course, the Americans had profited immensely from their study of the philosophers of the Scottish Enlightenment, but the Americans' opportunities and challenges, and their combined political genius, took them far beyond their Scottish teachers in the realm of political thought. Hutcheson, Smith, Reid, and their colleagues provided the American Founders with many of the ideas and arguments that inspired them, but you won't find the Founders' political theories within the Scottish Enlightenment.

Nor were the Founders' political theories determined by what they learned from the Scots. The Founders' work is a unique integration and a new creation. They made brilliant use of the whole range of ideas and philosophical discoveries provided by their Scottish teachers, adapting those ideas to their urgent need, their enormous opportunity, and their noble purpose of establishing a system of liberty. Along the way, in the astonishing burst of brilliance that is *The Federalist Papers*, they also accomplished what had eluded even the towering genius of Adam Smith.

The Founders thought and built anew. The world-changing contributions to political thought found in the Declaration and *The Federalist Papers*, and embodied in the Constitution, are the work of the Founders and the gifts of the American Enlightenment.

What then of the Tocqueville quote? Since neither sentence stands up to scrutiny, here is a corrected version:

> The American Founders were the boldest political thinkers of the eighteenth-century, and they also succeeded in putting their political theories effectively into practice in America. And because the Founders were also strong champions of religion and of religious liberty, by the time of Tocqueville's visit anti-religious doctrines had never made any headway in America.

SEVEN

Turning Away from the Founders

"Many of us today reject the universal and timeless claims of the Declaration, and therefore also we reject the forms of government established in the Constitution. We follow the notion, born among academics, that no such claim can be true and no such form can abide. This belief is very strong among Americans now, and it has made vast achievements in changing our government."
—LARRY ARNN, THE FOUNDERS' KEY

☙

WOODROW WILSON

*"Justly revered as our great Constitution is, it could be stripped off
and thrown aside like a garment, and the nation would still stand
forth in the living vestment of flesh and sinew, warm with the
heart-blood of one people, ready to recreate constitutions and laws."*
—WOODROW WILSON

Our Constitution is justly revered, but not by Wilson. He really
did want to cast our charter of liberty aside. Wilson's progressivism
was all about progressing beyond the Founders' ideas.

Our presidents take an oath to preserve, protect and defend
the Constitution. Lincoln believed that he was bound by that
oath to "face the arithmetic" of a bloody Civil War. Yet only a few
decades later, Wilson is eager to rid America of the Constitution
of the Founders. How did this happen?

You can go a long way toward understanding the history of
our Constitution by examining the lives of just two men, John
Witherspoon and Woodrow Wilson. Both men were powerful
agents of change and, at the same time, great symbols of the
intellectual currents of their times. In addition, they have story
lines with astonishing parallels. Both were president of Princeton,
transforming it by importing a model of the university from
Europe, both had a powerful impact on the direction of American
politics by their writing and speaking, and for both Princeton was
a springboard to positions of political eminence.

As a teacher and a political leader, John Witherspoon had an
impact on the Constitution that is almost impossible to overestimate. In the words of John Adams, "he is as high a Son of Liberty,
as any man in America." A Scot, educated at Edinburgh, a student

of Adam Smith and Thomas Reid, he brought the ideas of the Scottish Enlightenment to Princeton, and re-made Princeton on the Scottish model of the university. A signer of the Declaration of Independence and a hard-working member of the Continental Congress, he is the perfect symbol of the impact of the Scottish Enlightenment on the Founders and the Founding.

If you want to understand the political assault on the Constitution during the course of the twentieth century, the place to start is with Woodrow Wilson. Wilson too re-made Princeton, this time on the model of the German university. He was a disciple of the German philosopher G. W. F. Hegel. Hegel exalted the state and rejected the idea of individual liberty. By championing Hegel, Wilson played a leading role in introducing a German strain of thought into the American body politic that was alien to the self-evident truths and the unalienable rights of the Founders.

According to Hegel, the process of history itself renders the ideas of each earlier period obsolete. Therefore, according to Hegel and to Wilson, the Founders' propositions were only relevant to the time of the Founders. Simply because history had moved on, those propositions had been rendered obsolete; they had appeared to the Founders to be self-evident only because the Founders lived in the historical era they lived in.

As crazy as that sounds, that really was the argument. There was no need for Wilson or for anyone to demolish the Founders' self-evident truths; history itself had—somehow—done the work, or, rather, made it unnecessary for anyone to do the work. The Founders' ideas were merely ideas of and for another time.

Despite Hegel's enormous influence, his argument is afflicted by an evident logical fallacy. Instead of being self-evident, it is apparently self-refuting. Consider this formulation of his argument:

"No proposition is absolutely true; all propositions are only relative to the historical period of the originator of the proposition." If we assume the proposition is true, it follows that it is not true—but only relative to the historical period of its originator!

H egel's doctrine of history spawned a family of theories. The general name for them is "historicism." Because there are many varieties of historicism, in order to be clear about which one is being referred to it is often useful to be specific, as in "Hegel's historicism" or "Marx's historicism." Wilson's progressivism was one variety. Stalin and Hitler had their own versions, and their versions had much in common. Here is Richard Overy in his book *The Dictators*:

> "The two dictatorships justified a moral outlook that *rejected universal truths* or values by asserting that the moral order [claimed by the dictatorship] was legitimized *by the higher necessity of history* . . . the two dictatorships constructed moral orders that preached the absolute value of the collective and the absolute obligation to abandon concern for self in the name of the whole." [Emphasis added]

Hitler and Stalin each claimed the process of history had done away with "universal truths or values", and as a result of that process, absolutism had made its return.

During the early period of the careers of Hitler and Stalin and soon after Wilson's presidency, Calvin Coolidge spoke in Philadelphia on the occasion of the 150th anniversary of the Declaration of Independence. He had this to say:

"It is often asserted that the world has made a great deal of progress since 1776, that we have had new thoughts and new experiences which have given us a great advance over the people of that day, and that we may therefore very well discard their conclusions for something more modern. But that reasoning can not be applied to this great charter. If all men are created equal, that is final. If they are endowed with inalienable rights, that is final. If governments derive their just powers from the consent of the governed, that is final. No advance, no progress can be made beyond these propositions. If anyone wishes to deny their truth or their soundness, the only direction in which he can proceed historically is not forward, but backward toward the time when there was no equality, no rights of the individual, no rule of the people. Those who wish to proceed in that direction can not lay claim to progress. They are reactionary. Their ideas are not more modern, but more ancient, than those of the Revolutionary fathers."

THE PROGRESSIVES: MODERN AND POSTMODERN

The Modern Progressives

"No doubt a great deal of nonsense has been talked about the inalienable rights of the individual, and a great deal that was mere vague sentiment and pleasing speculation has been put forward as fundamental principle . . . "

—WOODROW WILSON

Woodrow Wilson, the very model of the modern progressive, utterly rejected the Founders' self-evident truths and unalienable rights. Wilson and the modern progressives saw the Declaration and the Constitution as anachronisms that America needed to progress beyond.

Wilson based his rejection of the philosophy of the Founders on the philosophy of the nineteenth century German G. W. F. Hegel, writing:

> "[T]he philosophy of any time is, as Hegel says, 'nothing but the spirit of that time expressed in abstract thought.'"

For Wilson, history had moved on and, as a result, the thinking of the Founders had become, as he says in the above quote, "nonsense."

For Wilson and the modern progressives, the Constitutional limits on the power of government the Founders had so carefully crafted to protect our unalienable rights were actually defects. According to the progressives, those limits hobbled government, preventing it from using its powers to change society.

Although Wilson accomplished much, it was Franklin Roosevelt who succeeded in making the great leap forward to Big Government and a new vision of the relationship of the citizen and the government. In his speech to the Commonwealth Club in San Francisco in 1932 while still a candidate, he made this astonishing statement of his political vision:

> "Government is a relation of give and take, a contract, perforce, if we would follow the thinking out of which it grew. Under such a contract *rulers were accorded power*, and *the people*

consented to that power on consideration that they be *accorded certain rights. The task of statesmanship has always been the re-definition of these rights* in terms of a changing and growing social order." [Emphasis added]

FDR turned the principles of the Founders upside down. Gone are the unalienable rights of a sovereign people and a government whose purpose is protecting those unalienable rights. Instead, according to FDR, the American people have rulers. In FDR's version of politics, the American people surrender power to those rulers in order to gain rights. And, according to FDR, it is the task of the rulers to re-define the people's rights as they see fit "in terms of a changing and growing social order."

However, progressivism, ever progressing, did not stop there. It is a new time and the spirit of the new time has brought forth a new generation of progressives.

II. The Postmodern Progressives

"That depends on what the meaning of the word 'is' is."
—WILLIAM JEFFERSON CLINTON

The Democratic Party claims Thomas Jefferson as the first President of the party, yet it is clear that there is a big difference in the thinking of Thomas Jefferson and the recent President with "Jefferson" in his name—and even a big difference between the thinking of Woodrow Wilson and that recent President. Thomas Jefferson believed there are truths that are self-evident; Wilson rejected Jefferson's self-evident truths; FDR replaced Jefferson's self-evident truths with a totally different political doctrine;

Clinton's statement goes even beyond Wilson and FDR to invoke a challenge to the very possibility of truth.

According to the postmodernists, the meaning of "is"—and everything else—is up for grabs. As Jonah Goldberg wrote in an article in the magazine *National Review*, postmodernists hold "that truth is 'socially constructed,' so not only is there no capital-T Truth that stands outside the individual or society, but all meaning is up for grabs in a contest to see which 'stories' will define our civilization. Ultimately this means truth becomes a political question about who wields power rather than an investigation into anything eternal or external to our own perspectives."

The postmodernists go far beyond Hegel's rejectionism to deny even the meaningfulness of claims to truth. The French postmodernist Michel Foucault puts their position this way:

> "It is meaningless to speak in the name of—or against—Reason, Truth or Knowledge."

Richard Rorty, the best known of the American postmodernists, makes the same point with greater apparent philosophical rigor:

> "To say that we should drop the idea of truth as out there waiting to be discovered is not to say that we have discovered that, out there, there is no truth. It is to say that our purposes would be served best by ceasing to see truth . . . as a topic of philosophical interest, or 'true' as a term which repays 'analysis.'"

Postmodernism is philosophy cut loose from common sense and proud of it.

In his excellent book, *Explaining Postmodernism*, Professor Stephen Hicks presents a list of claims of postmodern discourse, primarily to make the philosophical point that the claims are self-contradictory. Of course, given the premises of postmodernism, the fact that they are self-contradictory is not a problem for the postmodernists.

- On the one hand, all cultures are equally deserving of respect; on the other, Western culture is uniquely destructive and bad.
- Values are subjective—but sexism and racism are really evil.
- Technology is bad and destructive—and it is unfair that some people have more technology than others.
- Tolerance is good and dominance is bad—but when postmodernists come to power, political correctness follows, and opposing views are not tolerated.

Clearly, these claims are very different from the self-evident truths of Jefferson and the Founders, and these ideas would not have made sense even to Woodrow Wilson.

The invasion of the postmodernists came in the second half of the twentieth century, about a century after the Hegelian tide. As you may have heard, the postmodernists have captured the commanding heights of academia. Once again, as did the Hegelians, they first successfully invaded academia, and then reached out to change American society and government.

While the modern progressives primarily oppose the constitutional limits on government power and as a result seek to dismantle the Constitutional order, the postmodern progressives have a much more radical, far-reaching and often confusing agenda. This difference tends to make the two versions of progressivism fairly easy to distinguish.

Modern progressivism, rejecting the Constitutional safeguards of individual liberty in favor of the government's ability to bring about social change, favors an ever expanding and activist role for government in society, such as government control of health care, government intervention in the economy and so on.

In contrast, postmodern progressivism is not content merely to dismantle the American Constitution; many of its proposals—such as laws mandating that public-school students be allowed to use the restrooms and locker rooms of the gender they identify with—seem intended to defy common sense, as if postmodern progressivism recognizes that common sense is its real enemy.

Other proposals of postmodern progressives aim at getting beyond American national sovereignty. In that sense, American postmodern progressivism is post-American also, seeking to give power to international or supra-national bodies like the United Nations and to introduce *sharia* (Islamic law) and the constitutional law of foreign nations into American jurisprudence. Postmodern progressives also welcome illegal immigration, and they embrace international efforts to address global problems such as climate, seemingly as much because of the international form of the response as because of concern about the problem to be addressed.

EIGHT

Common Sense Nation

"Common Sense Realism was virtually the official creed of the American Republic . . . "

—Arthur Herman

COMMON SENSE NATION

"Common Sense Realism was virtually the official creed of the American Republic. So what was it? Its founder, Thomas Reid . . . made an important alteration to Locke's theories. Reid said that the mind is not an entirely blank tabula rasa [Locke's sheet of blank paper] but comes equipped with a . . . power of judgment [Reid called] common sense."

—ARTHUR HERMAN, *THE CAVE AND THE LIGHT*

This quote of Professor Herman points the way to the path we have followed together to understand the Founders.

As we have seen, Reid and his Scottish colleagues deeply informed the Founders' deliberations. According to Jeffry Morrison, this philosophical tradition reigned supreme in America for more than 150 years. That was true both within academia and in American society outside of academia as well.

In the years after the Founding era, common sense realism became ever more ingrained in the American character and the American way of thinking. It was studied and taught in American colleges, and its precepts pervaded American society. It was the coin of the realm in American thinking.

Perhaps the most powerful illustration of this is the utterly astonishing fact of Abraham Lincoln. If the largely self-educated Lincoln was a supreme master of common sense reasoning and moral logic in politics, as he surely was, then isn't the fact that America could produce such a man and then elect him to lead the nation rich in implications? The ways of thinking which the Founders had embodied in the Declaration and in the Constitution had over time permeated America, making Lincoln's life, election and legacy possible.

Yet in his book *Democracy in America*, Alexis de Tocqueville wrote,

> "I think that in no country in the civilized world is less attention paid to philosophy than in the United States."

You can find this statement quoted very frequently in books and articles about America. In fact, it is about as frequently quoted as the other Tocqueville passage we examined earlier. And just as with the earlier passage, it nearly always goes unchallenged. Here is that earlier one again so that we can examine them side-by-side:

> "There is no country in the world in which the boldest political theories of the eighteenth-century philosophers are put so effectively into practice as in America."

The two statements even share the same "there is no country in the world" format—and yet they point in opposite directions. Are we to believe the country which pays the least attention to philosophy is also the country which applies philosophers' ideas most effectively?

Once again Tocqueville has given us a ringing declaration about America which does an excellent job of sending the unwary reader—and surprising numbers of unwary scholars—off in the wrong direction.

Although Tocqueville, as we have seen, was in error about which eighteenth-century philosophers' theories had been applied "so boldly and effectively" that claim, with all its problems, is closer to the truth about America.

At the time of the Founding and still at the time of Tocqueville's visit in 1831, America could in fairness be said to be the preeminently philosophical nation. America was dedicated to a philosophical truth, the proposition that all men are created equal. That truth, the design of the Constitution, and the Founders' vision for how American society and the American economy are to operate were grounded in the common sense realism of the American Enlightenment. America, the common sense nation, was the one nation in the world fully prepared and capable of applying philosophical theories boldly and effectively.

Perhaps the most dramatic illustration of this aspect of American exceptionalism is this: *The Federalist Papers*—America's most important book of political theory and, I would argue, the world's most important work in the political theory of liberty—was originally published in serial form in American *newspapers*. They were read and keenly debated by Americans in every walk of life. I invite you to pause for a moment to ponder that astonishing fact. The American citizens' debate on the proposed Constitution was political debate on a very high level indeed.

But despite its deep roots in American society and thought, common sense realism, both in academia and in society, began to be successfully challenged in America during the second half of the nineteenth century.

What could possibly have occurred to make so great a change possible? Perhaps only a very great trauma to the American body politic could have created the conditions required for such a fundamental change. We do not have to search very far to find such a trauma. The American republic survived the Civil War but did so at a terrible cost.

The political problem of slavery led one region of America to declare that it was a new nation dedicated to the *rejection* of the proposition Lincoln said America is dedicated to. Alexander Stephens, the Vice-President of the Confederacy, said this in a famous speech at the outset:

> "The corner stone of our new government rests upon the great truth that the negro is not equal to the white man; that slavery, subordination to the superior race, is his natural and normal condition. Our new government is the first in the history of the world based upon this great physical, philosophical, and moral truth."

After the war, Stephens eventually returned to the U.S. House of Representatives as a Democrat from Georgia, and was re-elected to the House four more times.

How the Civil War damaged the "official creed of the American republic" and how other factors may have contributed to its decline thereafter are topics for another book and a different author. It is, however, interesting to note that Woodrow Wilson had lived in the Confederacy as a boy and had prayed for a Southern victory. He later often spoke of having seen Confederate president Jefferson Davis marched through Augusta Georgia in chains and Robert E. Lee pass by under Union guard after his surrender.

In any event, for our purposes, we need to note that in academia common sense realism was eclipsed by a new philosophy called "pragmatism" around the beginning of the twentieth century. This change in academia occurred during the same period in which progressivism was rising to prominence in politics.

According to Allen Guelzo, the American philosophical tradition which descended directly from the era of the Founders had fallen victim to a failure by its proponents to adapt to the new system of politics within academia. Academic associations of specialists such as the American Philosophical Association and the American Political Science Association, founded around the beginning of the twentieth century, rapidly rose to prominence and came to dominate their respective academic disciplines. The common sense realist professors were swept aside by the new system. As a result, common sense realism lost out to pragmatism, and to an astonishing degree given its once unrivaled preeminence in America, was almost forgotten.

On the surface, replacing common sense realism with pragmatism might not seem that consequential. After all, in our everyday speech, "common sense" and "pragmatic" are commonly used almost interchangeably. But by defining truth as "what works" pragmatism struck a blow aimed directly at the thinking of the Founders and at American common sense realism. The American pragmatist William James made that clear in this famous statement in his book *The Meaning of Truth*:

> "The true is only the expedient in our way of thinking, just as the right is only the expedient in the way of our behaving."

In other words, for the pragmatist there are no self-evident truths and no unalienable rights.

The consequences were profound.

With common sense realism no longer taught and defended in academia, and progressivism powerfully advocated in the public arena, the American Enlightenment began to fade from memory, and many Americans began to lose their grip on the American Idea.

Cast adrift on the intellectual and political currents of the twentieth century, America has arrived at the present moment. Today, the Democratic Party, which claims to be the party of Jefferson although it would be more accurate to say that it is the party of Woodrow Wilson, rides roughshod over the Constitution, and the party of Lincoln struggles politically at least in part because the Founders' vision of liberty and limited government is no longer the shared vision of America's citizens.

Yet the common sense nation endures. It lives on in the brilliant common sense commentary of American thinkers such as Angelo Codevilla and Thomas Sowell and in the robust common sense of millions of American citizens.

NINE

A Brief History of "Liberalism"

"In the United States 'liberal' means today a set of ideas and political postulates that in every regard are the opposite of all that liberalism meant to the preceding generations. The American self-styled liberal aims at government omnipotence, is a resolute foe of free enterprise, and advocates all-round planning by the authorities . . . Every measure aiming at confiscating some of the assets of those who own more than the average or at restricting the rights of the owners of property is considered as liberal and progressive."

—LUDWIG VON MISES, *LIBERALISM*

The term "liberal" comes from the Latin "liber" meaning "free." Liberalism originally referred to the philosophy of liberty, that is, the philosophy of the American Founders and their tradition, the great tradition which inspired the Founders and which they did so much to define and advance.

In fact, if Freidrich Hayek is correct, the introduction of the term in its original sense has a very close historical link to the Founders. Hayek traces the introduction of the term "liberal" to its use by Adam Smith. Hayek points to such characteristic passages as this one in *The Wealth of Nations* where Smith wrote of "allowing every man to pursue his own interest his own way, upon the liberal plan of equality, liberty, and justice."

The term "liberal" today means the precise opposite of what it once meant. Using the original, classical meaning, Mises wrote:

> "As the liberal sees it, the task of the state consists solely and exclusively in guaranteeing the protection of life, health, liberty, and private property against violent attacks . . . Anti-liberal policies have so far expanded the functions of the state as to leave hardly any field of human activity free of government interference."

Yet the policies Mises refers to here as "anti-liberal" were actually labeled as liberal by their proponents.

So, we have a familiar word with two totally contrary meanings, one meaning having been very nearly completely buried by the other. How did this confusing state of affairs come about?

It was the result of a political master stroke by that shrewdest of politicians—Franklin Delano Roosevelt.

If you measure presidential success simply by the number of times a man is elected to the presidency, then FDR is the most successful American President. Elected four times, FDR held office continually until his death. His claim on the office attests to his astonishing ability to dominate the game of politics, and also demonstrates his willingness to break with the tradition established by Washington of retiring after a maximum of two terms.

But to understand the brilliance of his capture for his political purposes the term "liberal," we need to understand the challenge FDR faced and the opportunity that he seized.

PROGRESSIVISM

"Power tends to corrupt, and absolute power corrupts absolutely."
—LORD ACTON, 1834–1902

"I cannot imagine power as a thing negative and not positive."
—WOODROW WILSON, 1856–1924

Take a look at the two quotes above. The Acton quote may be familiar to you. It evokes the hard testimony of human history as revealed by Caligula, Louis XIV and Hitler.

As the noted scholar J. Rufus Fears has written, Lord Acton was "a thinker of supreme importance in the intellectual heritage of classical Liberalism." (Prof. Fears is here forced to use the phrase "classical Liberalism" because of the confused state of the term "liberalism." In Acton's day, it was simply called "Liberalism.") Acton's book *Essays in the History of Liberty* is one of the greatest works of scholarship of the nineteenth century.

Woodrow Wilson, of course, was the great champion of progressivism in American politics. It was Wilson who set the Democratic Party on the course that was to make it the party of progressivism. The Wilson quote, by the way, is from his book *Congressional Government*.

According to classical Liberalism, the problem of government is how to make it strong enough to do what government must do without encroaching on individual liberty. As we noted earlier, the dangerous nature of political power was uppermost in the minds of the Founders when they were debating the design of the Constitution.

The effect of power on human nature explains the Founders' focus on defining and limiting federal power. As we have seen, they did so by distributing power among the executive, legislative and judicial branches of the federal government, preserving the political independence of the states and creating a zone of liberty around the individual—even by further dividing the legislative power itself, crafting two legislative bodies with separate powers and competing interests. The Founders' republic is the supreme achievement of classical Liberalism.

In one sense, the Acton quote states the obvious, but in a much more important sense, it stakes out a point of view. As Americans, it is easy for us to forget that our native perspective is not the perspective of all humankind. Today, we are told, many Russians still revere Stalin, even Russians who were alive during the horrors of the Stalin era. And among Muslims, even Muslims living in the West, there are vast numbers, perhaps even an overwhelming majority, who believe that self-rule by the people is a violation of their religion. These non-believers in the philosophy of liberty are not concerned about the bad effects of unchecked power on rulers or on countries or on the objectivity of thinkers infatuated with the idea of power.

Nor was Wilson. He claimed he was unable to imagine that power can be a negative thing. This is an astonishing claim, isn't it? One searches in vain in Wilson's writings for the persuasive (or even moderately compelling) refutation of the Founders' concern with the dangers of political power.

As strange as the Wilson quote is, it does as much for our understanding of progressivism as the Acton quote does for classical Liberalism. Wilson and his fellow progressives were trying to progress beyond the vision and the system of the Founders. Wilson rejected the Founders' philosophy of liberty and the Constitution which embodies that philosophy. According to Wilson, the Constitutional limits on the power of government the Founders had so carefully crafted were actually defects. Those limits hobbled government, preventing it from using the power of government to change America. Wilson's view of governmental power is in direct opposition to the view of Acton and the Founders, that is, of classical Liberalism.

According to Wilson, following Hegel, abstract principles do not survive from one historical period to the next. History had simply moved on, with the Constitution having outlived its time and, therefore, its claim to validity. But from a traditional American perspective, Hegel's doctrine gets even worse. The Founders put the focus on individual liberty; Hegel placed the state and its power at the center, writing that "all worth which the human being possesses—all spiritual reality, he possesses only through the State." For Hegel, the movement of the state through time was the "march of God on earth." Consequently, one "must worship the state as a terrestrial divinity." Hegel revered political power and idolized Napoleon.

Wilson came by his training in Hegel's ideas in the ordinary way—he learned them in college. During the second half of the nineteenth century German ideas were very much in fashion, and Johns Hopkins University, where Wilson got his Ph.D. in political science in 1886, was then an outpost of German thinking in America. Wilson's teachers at Johns Hopkins, and nearly every member of the faculty of the entire university, had been educated in Germany.

The Hitler nightmare was later to cause thoughtful people to reconsider the premises of German political thought, but prior to the Nazi atrocities, German political thinking was the latest thing. Wilson was German political thought's man in America, and he was impatient to change America in conformity to the German way of political thought and action.

Wilson's ambitions were not limited to overturning the Founders' ideas in academia. He wanted to get his hands on the levers of power. For that he needed a concrete political program, something Hegelian philosophy by itself does not provide. He also found this in Germany, and what he found was a far cry from the classical Liberal ideal.

American progressivism is identified with the welfare state, and the welfare state was the invention of Prince Otto von Bismarck (1815-1898), Germany's famously ruthless "Iron Chancellor." Bismarck considered Germans to be "children" of the Father State. Like Hegel, he considered the interests of the State to be paramount. According to Bismarck, the government was to arrange and direct the lives of individual Germans. His view of government was later on to be celebrated by Hitler and the Nazis, and it was Bismarck's *Wohlfahrtsstaat* (the welfare state) that was the inspiration for Wilson and Wilson's fellow progressives.

If you are surprised to learn of progressivism's roots in German philosophy and German political history, it is simply because for obvious reasons progressives eventually decided to conceal those roots.

LIBERALISM 2.0

FDR faced a challenge. Both he and Hitler came to power in 1933.

FDR was a proud progressive who had served in the Wilson administration. Yet he was elected in a time when progressivism's German roots, Wilson's open admiration for all things German, and Wilson's scorn for the Constitution, all had enormous potential to make political trouble for FDR and his party.

There were other purely domestic developments that had put progressivism in a bad light. Prohibition, enacted at the crest of the progressive wave in 1919 during Wilson's administration, had not exactly turned out to be a crowd pleaser. The country was in the Depression, making it painfully clear that the Federal Reserve, one of progressivism's crown jewels, had not in fact smoothed out the business cycle as promised. And progressivism's other prized accomplishment, the progressive income tax, was a sore point for many voters.

Time for a name change!

And what a change it was. Nowhere is FDR's genius for politics more evident than in his decision and his brilliant campaign to re-name progressivism as liberalism. A lesser politician could never have gotten away with it.

For the Democrats, the benefits were enormous. FDR managed to change the meaning of a word and to transform American political discourse with an impact stretching to our own time.

Think of it: FDR stole the label of the philosophy of liberty and bestowed it on the party of the state, the party of government, the self-proclaimed political enemies of classical Liberalism and of limited government. It was a knock-out punch that left the proponents of the philosophy of liberty without a name.

The blow was devastating to the defenders of the Constitution. What should they call themselves now? As my friend the eminent scholar Professor Charles Kesler writes in his masterful book *I Am the Change*:

> "FDR suggested, helpfully, that they ought to call themselves conservatives, a designation they were loath to accept because it sounded . . . vaguely un-American . . . Robert Taft, 'Mr. Conservative,' was still insisting he was a liberal in 1946."

The classical, Constitutional Liberals resisted taking FDR's helpful suggestion because "conservative" had always been the label of their political foes. As Jacques Barzun wrote, "free enterprise, free trade, freedom to vote and run for office, free speech and religion are Liberal achievements." Classical Liberalism's political opponents in the fight for liberty, the champions of the old order, had always, and very properly too, been called the "conservatives."

It gets confusing, doesn't it? That is the beauty of it from the progressives' point of view. Making sense about this has become a challenge even for very sensible people. Consider this passage written by Harvey Mansfield, the distinguished Harvard professor, in the pages of *The Claremont Review of Books*, America's fore-most journal of political thought:

> "A *true* liberal is at minimum a person who wants both sides to
> be heard. That is the practice of free speech and its companion,
> academic freedom. The *so-called* liberals today don't want to
> hear both sides. *Real* liberals . . . do, but those who stand
> up for liberalism today are mostly conservatives." [Emphasis
> added]

I cite this in complete sympathy with Professor Mansfield, noting only that this thoughtful scholar is forced to modify *liberal* with *true*, *so-called*, and *real* in quick succession in order to be able use *liberalism* without a modifier—all this, in order to make an important point which, however, has to be stated as an apparent paradox.

Political discourse in America, even when conducted by our very best, has been plunged into terminological confusion. This confusion has not been good for our republic, dependent as it is ultimately on the ability of the voters to make sound and prudent choices at the ballot box.

In the 1950s William F. Buckley and other leading American defenders of the Constitution decided to accede to FDR's "helpful" suggestion and call themselves conservatives. Their decision grew out of the failure of the proponents of the philosophy of liberty to mount a successful defense of their right to their own name. So it was that the name of liberalism became the property of the opponents of Liberalism.

At about the same time, in the 1950s, Leonard Read, founder of the Foundation for Economic Education, began calling himself a "libertarian." Like the word liberal, it was derived from the Latin *liber*, free. Over time, other proponents of the philosophy of liberty followed Read and embraced the label. Meanwhile, others were following Buckley's lead and calling themselves conservatives. The leading libertarian thinker David Boaz, like Professor Mansfield also struggling with the terminological tangles FDR engendered, takes up this issue in *The Libertarian Reader*:

> "Some old [classical] liberals began calling themselves conservatives. After all, what is conservatism in a liberal [progressive] society? If it means a defense of constitutional liberties and the private enterprise system, then 'conservatives' may in fact be conservative [classical] liberals."

FDR's successful gambit had broken American classical Liberalism in two, splitting the defenders of the philosophy of liberty into two distinct groups. Both defend the Constitution and the American private enterprise system, though they don't always agree. The libertarians put more emphasis on classical Liberal economics and the free market, while the proponents of the philosophy of liberty who now call themselves conservatives tend to put greater emphasis on the principles of the Declaration and the Constitution.

By creating the conditions that divided classical Liberalism, FDR made the way easier for progressivism's sweeping advance during the past century—and progressivism's success in transforming the shared assumptions of Americans has been simply astonishing. The Founders would be amazed and disheartened by the level of governmental coercion and taxation in America that is the result of progressivism's advance. In the words of Mises, writing before WWII and using the term "liberal" in its original sense:

> "In our age, in which anti-liberal ideas prevail, virtually everyone thinks accordingly, just as, a hundred years ago, most people thought in terms of the then prevailing liberal ideology."

FDR's capture of the term "liberalism" was a brilliant master stroke that greatly contributed to progressivism's phenomenal ascent in American politics.

And we must remember that the triumph of progressivism is the triumph of German political thought in America. Here is Leo Strauss in *Natural Right and History*, published in 1950:

> "About a generation ago, an American diplomat could still say that 'the natural and divine foundation of the rights of man . . . is self-evident to all Americans.' At about the same time a German scholar could still describe the difference between German thought and that of Western Europe and the United States by saying that the West still attached decisive importance to natural right, while in Germany the very terms 'natural right' and 'humanity' 'have now become almost incomprehensible.' . . . It would not be the first time that a nation, defeated on the battlefield . . . has deprived its conquerors of the most sublime fruit of victory by imposing on them the yoke of its own thought. . . . certainly American social science . . . is [now] dedicated to the proposition that all men are endowed by the evolutionary process or by a mysterious

fate with many kinds of urges and aspirations, but certainly with no natural right."

⚜

CONSERVATISM

"Conservatism proper is a legitimate, probably necessary, and certainly widespread attitude of opposition to drastic change."
—FREIDRICH HAYEK, *THE CONSTITUTION OF LIBERTY*

Any attempt to make sense of the meaning of liberalism simply must address conservatism. Both terms are generally understood in relation to each other. In the generally accepted image, they occupy different positions on a line, with the liberals on the left and the conservatives on the right. However, that picture is not accurate in our progressive era.

Before the progressive era, the classical Liberals successfully championing liberty were opposed by the conservatives who defended the old order. During the past century, the classical Liberal order of liberty, free markets and limited government has been in the process of being dismantled by the progressives. The conservatives are in their traditional role of resisting change, but today the powerful agents of change are the progressives and the direction of change is being set by progressivism, not by classical Liberalism.

Conservatism is fundamentally a disposition. It represents the political expression of caution or of the underappreciated virtue of prudence. Drastic, hasty change is likely to have unintended consequences, even terrible ones. Let us learn from the past, make change carefully, be on the lookout for unintended consequences, says the sober-minded and careful conservative. Ian Tuttle in his article "To Carry the Fire" in *National Review* puts an American conservative stance like this:

> "The whole edifice, built up painstakingly over the ages, is liable to be thrown down suddenly by bad men or bad luck, neither of which is ever in short supply . . . So we proceed with caution."

Probably every society and every time has its conservatives, with tenets specific to each society's history and circumstances. For example, English conservatives today might want to preserve the monarchy, the Church of England as the established church, and the British aristocracy. In the same way, it makes sense to label as "conservative" those Iranians who opposed the revolution that changed Iran from a monarchy to a radical Islamist theocracy or those Russians who long for the return of the Soviet Union, but to call them "conservative" is not to suggest that their political views are similar or that their views are similar to those of an American who is dedicated to the principles of the American Founders.

According to Hayek, whether British, Iranian, Russian, or American, the problem with conservatism is this:

> "It may succeed by its resistance to current tendencies in slowing down undesirable developments, but, since it does not indicate another direction, it cannot prevent their continuance. It has, for this reason, invariably been the fate of conservatism to be dragged along a path not of its own choosing."

Hayek's description does seem to capture the story of the last century in American politics—the progressives setting the agenda and the opposition dragged unwillingly along a path not of its own choosing.

B ut classical Liberalism and progressivism each do "indicate a direction." Because progressivism defined itself in opposition to classical Liberalism, progressivism and classical Liberalism can appropriately be visualized as occupying different positions on a line and situated opposite each other.

The progressives are all for change *of a certain kind*. Their purpose is to use government to change society. They want to use the power of a big and constantly expanding government to arrange and direct the lives of individual citizens to conform to progressivism's constantly changing ideas of what society should be. (Once they believed in prohibition and eugenics, today they believe in gay marriage and global warming. Who knows what tomorrow will bring?) As a result, they, like Woodrow Wilson, see government power as a good thing, especially when it is wholly or largely in their hands as it has been for much of the last century.

The classical Liberals support change and progress, too, even lots of both. For classical Liberals, liberty, not government power, is their polar star, and progress is the natural result of liberty. The Founders' classical Liberal vision was to keep government limited, stable, and dedicated to the protection of our rights *in order to allow innovation* to flourish spontaneously in an always advancing American society. In the words of H. B. Phillips:

> "In an advancing society, any restriction on liberty reduces the
> number of things tried and so reduces the rate of progress.
> In such a society freedom of action . . . will on the average
> serve the rest of us better than under any orders we know
> how to give."

As the very great Scottish Enlightenment philosopher Adam Ferguson, Professor of Moral Philosophy at the University of Edinburgh, explained in 1767,

> "nations stumble upon establishments, which are indeed *the result of human action, but not the execution of any human design* . . . the establishments of men . . . arose from successive improvements that were made, without any sense of their general effect; and they bring human affairs to a state of complication, which the greatest reach of capacity with which human nature was ever adorned, could not have projected." [Emphasis added]

One trouble, then, with the attempt to force change by governmental power is that it actually reduces the rate of progress. Enforcing progress from the top down impinges on personal liberty, and consequently impedes progress. It also often wreaks havoc, as we have seen recently with the many problems created by Obamacare.

Progressivism, for all its belief in itself as the most advanced thinking, is only a contemporary version of statism, the oldest idea in government. In this sense, Adam Smith wrote about the progressive in his *Theory of Moral Sentiments* long before Woodrow Wilson began coming up with progressivism:

> "The man of system is apt to be very wise in his own conceit; and is often so enamoured with the supposed beauty of his own ideal plan of government, that he cannot suffer the smallest deviation from any part of it. He goes on to establish it completely and

in all its parts, without any regard either to the great interests, or to the strong prejudices which may oppose it. He seems to imagine that he can arrange the different members of a great society with as much ease as the hand arranges the different pieces upon a chess–board. He does not consider that . . . in the great chess-board of human society, every single piece has a principle of motion of its own, altogether different from that which the legislature might chuse to impress upon it. If those two principles coincide and act in the same direction, the game of human society will go on easily and harmoniously, and is very likely to be happy and successful. If they are opposite or different, the game will go on miserably, and the society must be at all times in the highest degree of disorder."

Over the course of the last century, the progressives have managed to install most of the changes they had originally targeted. As our government has grown ever larger and inserted itself into every area of life, our society suffers the inevitable results, the disorder Smith explains in the *Moral Sentiments* and the economic stasis he explains in *The Wealth of Nations*.

From the perspective of classical Liberalism, progressivism has added a mountain of follies under the burden of which our society and our economy now labor. For the classical Liberal, as Hayek wrote, "the chief need is . . . to free the process of spontaneous growth from the obstacles and encumbrances that human folly has erected."

If America chooses to head again in the direction of a truly liberal society and of limited government, there will be much to undo, and a bountiful harvest of progress to be gained. The Founders' wisdom is there to guide us. We only need to rediscover, recover, and reclaim it.

POSTSCRIPT

How to Misunderstand the Founders

"It was then [during the administration of Andrew Jackson] that it first became clear that, despite similarities of form, representative government in America was not to be an imitation of the English parliamentary system, and that, though the vocabulary of the Constitution may be that of the French Enlightenment, its American meaning is quite distinct."
—W. H. AUDEN, *THE DYER'S HAND*

Auden was a great poet. He spoke with real authority on poetry and literature, and in these comments about America he certainly *sounds* like an authority.

Yet he got it spectacularly wrong, didn't he? As you know, representative government in America was never an imitation of the English parliamentary system, nor was the Constitution written in the vocabulary of the French Enlightenment—and that was perfectly clear from the beginning. Three strikes and you are out.

I quote Auden as a reminder that we are likely to encounter pronouncements about America almost anywhere. Read an article or a book on any subject, even, as in this case, one on poetry and literature, and you may find that you are being presented with the author's view of America. You will, I predict, be astonished from now on by how often these pronouncements are mistaken, misguided, or misleading.

In trying to explain America by reference to the English parliamentary system and the French Enlightenment, Auden makes what we can call the Standard Error: offering an explanation of the American idea that leaves out the American Enlightenment.

APPENDIX I

Suggested Reading

Common Sense, by Thomas Paine

The Federalist Papers, Signet Classic
  Introduction and Notes by Charles R. Kesler, Edited by Clinton
Rossiter.

John Witherspoon and the Founding of the American Republic,
by Jeffry H. Morrison
  A very readable, enlightening, and informative biography of
a Founder who was at the center of the action in the American
Founding and in the American Enlightenment.
  If you are going to read on about the Founding, this is a great
place to start. Occasional generalizations about the Founding
aren't quite accurate though. See for one example the section
"Jefferson and Locke" above. For another example, the chapter
"Plain Common Sense" includes this sentence: "There was not a
man among them [the Founders]—not Jefferson, not Franklin,
not even the cerebral Madison, certainly not Washington—who
was a truly original political thinker or profound philosopher in

his own right." The "or" gives us two sentences, one probably correct but not surprising, the other quite misleading. A claim that no Founder was a profound philosopher would generally go unchallenged, but who would make that claim? None of the Founders wrote works in moral theory or theory of knowledge as Hutcheson or Reid had done. However, the claim that no Founder was an original political thinker does invite a challenge, certainly by me. See the chapter "Common Sense Nation" above.

The Roads to Modernity: The British, French, and American Enlightenments, by Gertrude Himmelfarb

See "Sorting Out the Enlightenments" above for a discussion of this very readable book.

How Adam Smith Can Change Your Life: An Unexpected Guide to Human Nature and Human Happiness, by Russ Roberts

Roberts has made Adam Smith's other masterpiece, *The Theory of Moral Sentiments,* completely accessible and completely understandable. In doing so, he has provided us with a profoundly revealing examination of the theory of human nature according to the American Founders: man the social being, endowed with moral sentiments, with a moral sense. The Founders were focused on their political enterprise, not moral philosophy, but Smith's ideas, beautifully expressed by Roberts, provide us with deep insight into the vision of human nature the Founders shared.

The Constitution of Liberty, by Friedrich A. Hayek

One of the greatest and most profound books of the twentieth century, *The Constitution of Liberty* makes a modern philosophical case for the classical Liberalism of the Founders.

This challenging and rewarding work is not an easy read. It has over 400 pages of text and many pages of thought-provoking footnotes.

SUGGESTED READING FOR LIBERALISM
Liberalism: The Classical Tradition, by Ludwig von Mises

Woodrow Wilson and the Roots of Modern Liberalism, by Ronald J. Pestritto

I Am the Change: Barack Obama and the Crisis of Liberalism, by Charles R. Kesler

Suggested Reading for the Scottish Enlightenment
How the Scots Invented the Modern World, by Arthur Herman
This fascinating book is a joy to read. Highly recommended.

The Library of Scottish Philosophy, series editor Gordon Graham
A really magnificent resource, dedicated to making the writings of Scottish philosophers accessible to modern readers.

SUGGESTED READING FOR RELIGION
AND THE AMERICAN FOUNDING
On Two Wings: Humble Faith and Common Sense at the American Founding, by Michael Novak
If you want to learn more about the importance of religious faith and religious learning to the American Founding, then this

is the book for you. Curiously, despite the reference to common sense in the subtitle, common sense gets little attention—and Thomas Reid is not even mentioned! Consequently, *Common Sense Nation* makes a useful companion to *On Two Wings*.

Seven Miracles That Saved America, by Chris Stewart and Ted Stewart

If you are interested in further exploring the role of Divine Providence in American history, then this is the book for you. Warning: the authors really believe in miracles.

APPENDIX II

The Declaration of Independence

IN CONGRESS, July 4, 1776.

The unanimous Declaration of the thirteen united States of America,

When in the Course of human events, it becomes necessary for one people to dissolve the political bands which have connected them with another, and to assume among the powers of the earth, the separate and equal station to which the Laws of Nature and of Nature's God entitle them, a decent respect to the opinions of mankind requires that they should declare the causes which impel them to the separation.

We hold these truths to be self-evident, that all men are created equal, that they are endowed by their Creator with certain unalienable Rights, that among these are Life, Liberty and the pursuit of Happiness. —That to secure these rights, Governments are instituted among Men, deriving their just powers from the consent of the governed, —That whenever any Form of Government becomes destructive of these ends, it is the Right of the People to alter or to abolish it, and to institute new Government, laying its foundation on such principles and organizing its powers in such form, as to them shall seem most likely to effect their Safety and Happiness. Prudence, indeed, will dictate that Governments long established should not be changed for light and transient causes; and accordingly all experience hath shewn, that mankind are more disposed to suffer, while evils are sufferable, than to right themselves by abolishing the forms to which they are accustomed. But when a long train of abuses and usurpations, pursuing invariably the same Object evinces a design to reduce them under absolute Despotism, it is their right, it is their duty, to throw off such Government, and to provide new Guards for their future security. —Such has been the patient sufferance of these Colonies; and such is now the necessity which constrains them to alter their former Systems of Government. The history of the present King of Great Britain is a history of repeated injuries and usurpations, all having in direct object the establishment of an absolute Tyranny over these States. To prove this, let Facts be submitted to a candid world.

He has refused his Assent to Laws, the most wholesome and necessary for the public good.

He has forbidden his Governors to pass Laws of immediate and pressing importance, unless suspended in their operation till his Assent should be obtained; and when so suspended, he has utterly neglected to attend to them.

He has refused to pass other Laws for the accommodation of large districts of people, unless those people would relinquish the right of Representation in the Legislature, a right inestimable to them and formidable to tyrants only.

He has called together legislative bodies at places unusual, uncomfortable, and distant from the depository of their public Records, for the sole purpose of fatiguing them into compliance with his measures.

He has dissolved Representative Houses repeatedly, for opposing with manly firmness his invasions on the rights of the people.

He has refused for a long time, after such dissolutions, to cause others to be elected; whereby the Legislative powers, incapable of Annihilation, have returned to the People at large for their exercise; the State remaining in the mean time exposed to all the dangers of invasion from without, and convulsions within.

He has endeavoured to prevent the population of these States; for that purpose obstructing the Laws for Naturalization of Foreigners; refusing to pass others to encourage their migrations hither, and raising the conditions of new Appropriations of Lands.

He has obstructed the Administration of Justice, by refusing his Assent to Laws for establishing Judiciary powers.

He has made Judges dependent on his Will alone, for the tenure of their offices, and the amount and payment of their salaries.

He has erected a multitude of New Offices, and sent hither swarms of Officers to harrass our people, and eat out their substance.

He has kept among us, in times of peace, Standing Armies without the Consent of our legislatures.

He has affected to render the Military independent of and superior to the Civil power.

He has combined with others to subject us to a jurisdiction foreign to our constitution, and unacknowledged by our laws; giving his Assent to their Acts of pretended Legislation:

For Quartering large bodies of armed troops among us:

For protecting them, by a mock Trial, from punishment for any Murders which they should commit on the Inhabitants of these States:

For cutting off our Trade with all parts of the world:

For imposing Taxes on us without our Consent:

For depriving us in many cases, of the benefits of Trial by Jury:

For transporting us beyond Seas to be tried for pretended offences

For abolishing the free System of English Laws in a neighbouring Province, establishing therein an Arbitrary government, and enlarging its Boundaries so as to render it at once an example and fit instrument for introducing the same absolute rule into these Colonies:

For taking away our Charters, abolishing our most valuable Laws, and altering fundamentally the Forms of our Governments:

For suspending our own Legislatures, and declaring themselves invested with power to legislate for us in all cases whatsoever.

He has abdicated Government here, by declaring us out of his Protection and waging War against us.

He has plundered our seas, ravaged our Coasts, burnt our towns, and destroyed the lives of our people.

He is at this time transporting large Armies of foreign Mercenaries to compleat the works of death, desolation and tyranny, already begun with circumstances of Cruelty & perfidy scarcely paralleled in the most barbarous ages, and totally unworthy the Head of a civilized nation.

He has constrained our fellow Citizens taken Captive on the high Seas to bear Arms against their Country, to become the executioners of their friends and Brethren, or to fall themselves by their Hands.

He has excited domestic insurrections amongst us, and has endeavoured to bring on the inhabitants of our frontiers, the merciless Indian Savages, whose known rule of warfare, is an undistinguished destruction of all ages, sexes and conditions.

In every stage of these Oppressions We have Petitioned for Redress in the most humble terms: Our repeated Petitions have been answered only by repeated injury. A Prince whose character is thus marked by every act which may define a Tyrant, is unfit to be the ruler of a free people.

Nor have We been wanting in attentions to our Brittish brethren. We have warned them from time to time of attempts by their legislature to extend an unwarrantable jurisdiction over us. We have reminded them of the circumstances of our emigration and settlement here. We have appealed to their native justice and magnanimity, and we have conjured them by the ties of our common kindred to disavow these usurpations, which, would inevitably interrupt our connections and correspondence. They too have been deaf to the voice of justice and of consanguinity. We must, therefore, acquiesce in the necessity, which denounces our Separation, and hold them, as we hold the rest of mankind, Enemies in War, in Peace Friends.

We, therefore, the Representatives of the united States of America, in General Congress, Assembled, appealing to the Supreme Judge of the world for the rectitude of our intentions, do, in the Name, and by Authority of the good People of these Colonies, solemnly publish and declare, That these United Colonies are, and of Right ought to be Free and Independent States; that they are Absolved from all Allegiance to the British Crown, and that all political connection between them and the State of

Great Britain, is and ought to be totally dissolved; and that as Free and Independent States, they have full Power to levy War, conclude Peace, contract Alliances, establish Commerce, and to do all other Acts and Things which Independent States may of right do. And for the support of this Declaration, with a firm reliance on the protection of divine Providence, we mutually pledge to each other our Lives, our Fortunes and our sacred Honor.

New Hampshire: Josiah Bartlett, William Whipple, Matthew Thornton

Massachusetts: John Hancock, Samuel Adams, John Adams, Robert Treat Paine, Elbridge Gerry

Rhode Island: Stephen Hopkins, William Ellery

Connecticut: Roger Sherman, Samuel Huntington, William Williams, Oliver Wolcott

New York: William Floyd, Philip Livingston, Francis Lewis, Lewis Morris

New Jersey: Richard Stockton, John Witherspoon, Francis Hopkinson, John Hart, Abraham Clark

Pennsylvania: Robert Morris, Benjamin Rush, Benjamin Franklin, John Morton, George Clymer, James Smith, George Taylor, James Wilson, George Ross

Delaware: Caesar Rodney, George Read, Thomas McKean

Maryland: Samuel Chase, William Paca, Thomas Stone, Charles Carroll of Carrollton

Virginia: George Wythe, Richard Henry Lee, Thomas Jefferson, Benjamin Harrison, Thomas Nelson, Jr., Francis Lightfoot Lee, Carter Braxton

North Carolina: William Hooper, Joseph Hewes, John Penn

South Carolina: Edward Rutledge, Thomas Heyward, Jr., Thomas Lynch, Jr., Arthur Middleton

Georgia: Button Gwinnett, Lyman Hall, George Walton

APPENDIX III

The Constitution of the United States of America

We the People of the United States, in Order to form a more perfect Union, establish Justice, insure domestic Tranquility, provide for the common defence, promote the general Welfare, and secure the Blessings of Liberty to ourselves and our Posterity, do ordain and establish this Constitution for the United States of America.

ARTICLE. I.

Section. 1.

All legislative Powers herein granted shall be vested in a Congress of the United States, which shall consist of a Senate and House of Representatives.

Section. 2.

The House of Representatives shall be composed of Members chosen every second Year by the People of the several States, and the Electors in each State shall have the Qualifications requisite for Electors of the most numerous Branch of the State Legislature.

No Person shall be a Representative who shall not have attained to the Age of twenty five Years, and been seven Years a Citizen of the United States, and who shall not, when elected, be an Inhabitant of that State in which he shall be chosen.

Representatives and direct Taxes shall be apportioned among the several States which may be included within this Union, according to their respective Numbers, which shall be determined by adding to the whole Number of free Persons, including those bound to Service for a Term of Years, and excluding Indians not taxed, three fifths of all other Persons. The actual Enumeration shall be made within three Years after the first Meeting of the Congress of the United States, and within every subsequent Term of ten Years, in such Manner as they shall by Law direct. The Number of Representatives shall not exceed one for every thirty Thousand, but each State shall have at Least one Representative; and until such enumeration shall be made, the State of New Hampshire shall be entitled to chuse three, Massachusetts eight, Rhode-Island and Providence Plantations one, Connecticut five, New-York six, New Jersey four, Pennsylvania eight, Delaware one, Maryland six, Virginia ten, North Carolina five, South Carolina five, and Georgia three.

When vacancies happen in the Representation from any State, the Executive Authority thereof shall issue Writs of Election to fill such Vacancies.

The House of Representatives shall chuse their Speaker and other Officers; and shall have the sole Power of Impeachment.
Section. 3.

The Senate of the United States shall be composed of two Senators from each State, chosen by the Legislature thereof, for six Years; and each Senator shall have one Vote.

Immediately after they shall be assembled in Consequence of the first Election, they shall be divided as equally as may be into three Classes. The Seats of the Senators of the first Class shall be vacated at the Expiration of the second Year, of the second Class at the Expiration of the fourth Year, and of the third Class at the Expiration of the sixth Year, so that one third may be chosen every second Year; and if Vacancies happen by Resignation, or otherwise, during the Recess of the Legislature of any State, the Executive thereof may make temporary Appointments until the next Meeting of the Legislature, which shall then fill such Vacancies.

No Person shall be a Senator who shall not have attained to the Age of thirty Years, and been nine Years a Citizen of the United States, and who shall not, when elected, be an Inhabitant of that State for which he shall be chosen.

The Vice President of the United States shall be President of the Senate, but shall have no Vote, unless they be equally divided.

The Senate shall chuse their other Officers, and also a President pro tempore, in the Absence of the Vice President, or when he shall exercise the Office of President of the United States.

The Senate shall have the sole Power to try all Impeachments. When sitting for that Purpose, they shall be on Oath or Affirmation. When the President of the United States is tried, the Chief Justice shall preside: And no Person shall be convicted without the Concurrence of two thirds of the Members present.

Judgment in Cases of Impeachment shall not extend further than to removal from Office, and disqualification to hold and enjoy any Office of honor, Trust or Profit under the United States: but the Party convicted shall nevertheless be liable and subject to Indictment, Trial, Judgment and Punishment, according to Law.

Section. 4.

The Times, Places and Manner of holding Elections for Senators and Representatives, shall be prescribed in each State by the Legislature thereof; but the Congress may at any time by Law make or alter such Regulations, except as to the Places of chusing Senators.

The Congress shall assemble at least once in every Year, and such Meeting shall be on the first Monday in December, unless they shall by Law appoint a different Day.

Section. 5.

Each House shall be the Judge of the Elections, Returns and Qualifications of its own Members, and a Majority of each shall constitute a Quorum to do Business; but a smaller Number may adjourn from day to day, and may be authorized to compel the Attendance of absent Members, in such Manner, and under such Penalties as each House may provide.

Each House may determine the Rules of its Proceedings, punish its Members for disorderly Behaviour, and, with the Concurrence of two thirds, expel a Member.

Each House shall keep a Journal of its Proceedings, and from time to time publish the same, excepting such Parts as may in their Judgment require Secrecy; and the Yeas and Nays of the Members of either House on any question shall, at the Desire of one fifth of those Present, be entered on the Journal.

Neither House, during the Session of Congress, shall, without the Consent of the other, adjourn for more than three days, nor to any other Place than that in which the two Houses shall be sitting.

Section. 6.

The Senators and Representatives shall receive a Compensation for their Services, to be ascertained by Law, and paid out of the Treasury of the United States. They shall in all Cases, except Treason, Felony and Breach of the Peace, be privileged from Arrest during their Attendance at the Session of their respective Houses, and in going to and returning from the same; and for any Speech or Debate in either House, they shall not be questioned in any other Place.

No Senator or Representative shall, during the Time for which he was elected, be appointed to any civil Office under the Authority of the United States, which shall have been created, or the Emoluments whereof shall have been encreased during such time; and no Person holding any Office under the United States, shall be a Member of either House during his Continuance in Office.

Section. 7.

All Bills for raising Revenue shall originate in the House of Representatives; but the Senate may propose or concur with Amendments as on other Bills.

Every Bill which shall have passed the House of Representatives and the Senate, shall, before it become a Law, be presented to the President of the United States; If he approve he shall sign it, but if not he shall return it, with his Objections to that House in which it shall have originated, who shall enter the Objections at large on their Journal, and proceed to reconsider it. If after such Reconsideration two thirds of that House shall agree to pass the Bill, it shall be sent, together with the Objections, to the other House, by which it shall likewise be reconsidered, and if approved by two thirds of that House, it shall become a Law. But in all such Cases the Votes of both Houses shall be determined by yeas and Nays, and the Names of the Persons voting for and against the Bill shall be entered on the Journal of each House respectively.

If any Bill shall not be returned by the President within ten Days (Sundays excepted) after it shall have been presented to him, the Same shall be a Law, in like Manner as if he had signed it, unless the Congress by their Adjournment prevent its Return, in which Case it shall not be a Law.

Every Order, Resolution, or Vote to which the Concurrence of the Senate and House of Representatives may be necessary (except on a question of Adjournment) shall be presented to the President of the United States; and before the Same shall take Effect, shall be approved by him, or being disapproved by him, shall be repassed by two thirds of the Senate and House of Representatives, according to the Rules and Limitations prescribed in the Case of a Bill.

Section. 8.

The Congress shall have Power To lay and collect Taxes, Duties, Imposts and Excises, to pay the Debts and provide for the common Defence and general Welfare of the United States; but all Duties, Imposts and Excises shall be uniform throughout the United States;

To borrow Money on the credit of the United States;

To regulate Commerce with foreign Nations, and among the several States, and with the Indian Tribes;

To establish an uniform Rule of Naturalization, and uniform Laws on the subject of Bankruptcies throughout the United States;

To coin Money, regulate the Value thereof, and of foreign Coin, and fix the Standard of Weights and Measures;

To provide for the Punishment of counterfeiting the Securities and current Coin of the United States;

To establish Post Offices and post Roads;

To promote the Progress of Science and useful Arts, by securing for limited Times to Authors and Inventors the exclusive Right to their respective Writings and Discoveries;

To constitute Tribunals inferior to the supreme Court;

To define and punish Piracies and Felonies committed on the high Seas, and Offences against the Law of Nations;

To declare War, grant Letters of Marque and Reprisal, and make Rules concerning Captures on Land and Water;

To raise and support Armies, but no Appropriation of Money to that Use shall be for a longer Term than two Years;

To provide and maintain a Navy;

To make Rules for the Government and Regulation of the land and naval Forces;

To provide for calling forth the Militia to execute the Laws of the Union, suppress Insurrections and repel Invasions;

To provide for organizing, arming, and disciplining, the Militia, and for governing such Part of them as may be employed in the Service of the United States, reserving to the States respectively, the Appointment of the Officers, and the Authority of training the Militia according to the discipline prescribed by Congress;

To exercise exclusive Legislation in all Cases whatsoever, over such District (not exceeding ten Miles square) as may, by Cession of particular States, and the Acceptance of Congress, become the Seat of the Government of the United States, and to exercise like Authority over all Places purchased by the Consent of the Legislature of the State in which the Same shall be, for the Erection of Forts, Magazines, Arsenals, dock-Yards, and other needful Buildings;—And

To make all Laws which shall be necessary and proper for carrying into Execution the foregoing Powers, and all other Powers vested by this Constitution in the Government of the United States, or in any Department or Officer thereof.
Section. 9.

The Migration or Importation of such Persons as any of the States now existing shall think proper to admit, shall not be prohibited by the Congress prior to the Year one thousand eight hundred and eight, but a Tax or duty may be imposed on such Importation, not exceeding ten dollars for each Person.

The Privilege of the Writ of Habeas Corpus shall not be suspended, unless when in Cases of Rebellion or Invasion the public Safety may require it.

No Bill of Attainder or ex post facto Law shall be passed.

No Capitation, or other direct, Tax shall be laid, unless in Proportion to the Census or enumeration herein before directed to be taken.

No Tax or Duty shall be laid on Articles exported from any State.

No Preference shall be given by any Regulation of Commerce or Revenue to the Ports of one State over those of another: nor shall Vessels bound to, or from, one State, be obliged to enter, clear, or pay Duties in another.

No Money shall be drawn from the Treasury, but in Consequence of Appropriations made by Law; and a regular Statement and Account of the Receipts and Expenditures of all public Money shall be published from time to time.

No Title of Nobility shall be granted by the United States: And no Person holding any Office of Profit or Trust under them, shall, without the Consent of the Congress, accept of any present, Emolument, Office, or Title, of any kind whatever, from any King, Prince, or foreign State.

Section. 10.

No State shall enter into any Treaty, Alliance, or Confederation; grant Letters of Marque and Reprisal; coin Money; emit Bills of Credit; make any Thing but gold and silver Coin a Tender in Payment of Debts; pass any Bill of Attainder, ex post facto Law, or Law impairing the Obligation of Contracts, or grant any Title of Nobility.

No State shall, without the Consent of the Congress, lay any Imposts or Duties on Imports or Exports, except what may be absolutely necessary for executing it's inspection Laws: and the net Produce of all Duties and Imposts, laid by any State on Imports or Exports, shall be for the Use of the Treasury of the United States; and all such Laws shall be subject to the Revision and Controul of the Congress.

No State shall, without the Consent of Congress, lay any Duty of Tonnage, keep Troops, or Ships of War in time of Peace, enter into any Agreement or Compact with another State, or with a foreign Power, or engage in War, unless actually invaded, or in such imminent Danger as will not admit of delay.

ARTICLE. II.

Section. 1.

The executive Power shall be vested in a President of the United States of America. He shall hold his Office during the Term of four Years, and, together with the Vice President, chosen for the same Term, be elected, as follows

Each State shall appoint, in such Manner as the Legislature thereof may direct, a Number of Electors, equal to the whole Number of Senators and Representatives to which the State may be entitled in the Congress: but no Senator or Representative, or Person holding an Office of Trust or Profit under the United States, shall be appointed an Elector.

The Electors shall meet in their respective States, and vote by Ballot for two Persons, of whom one at least shall not be an Inhabitant of the same State with themselves. And they shall make a List of all the Persons voted for, and of the Number of Votes for each; which List they shall sign and certify, and transmit sealed to the Seat of the Government of the United States, directed to the President of the Senate. The President of the Senate shall, in the Presence of the Senate and House of Representatives, open all the Certificates, and the Votes shall then be counted. The Person having the greatest Number of Votes shall be the President, if such Number be a Majority of the whole Number of Electors appointed; and if there be more than one who have such Majority, and have an equal Number of Votes, then the House of Representatives shall immediately chuse by Ballot one of them for President; and if no Person have a Majority, then from the five highest on the List the said House shall in like Manner chuse the President. But in chusing the President, the Votes shall be taken by States, the Representation from each State having one Vote; A quorum for this Purpose shall consist of a Member or Members from two thirds of the States, and a Majority of all the States shall be necessary to a Choice. In every Case, after the Choice of the President, the Person having the greatest Number of Votes of the Electors shall be the Vice President. But if there should remain two or more who have equal Votes, the Senate shall chuse from them by Ballot the Vice President.

The Congress may determine the Time of chusing the Electors, and the Day on which they shall give their Votes; which Day shall be the same throughout the United States.

No Person except a natural born Citizen, or a Citizen of the United States, at the time of the Adoption of this Constitution, shall be eligible to the Office of President; neither shall any Person be eligible to that Office who shall not have attained to the Age of thirty five Years, and been fourteen Years a Resident within the United States.

In Case of the Removal of the President from Office, or of his Death, Resignation, or Inability to discharge the Powers and Duties of the said Office, the Same shall devolve on the Vice President, and the Congress may by Law provide for the Case of Removal, Death, Resignation or Inability, both of the President and Vice President, declaring what Officer shall then act as President, and such Officer shall act accordingly, until the Disability be removed, or a President shall be elected.

The President shall, at stated Times, receive for his Services, a Compensation, which shall neither be encreased nor diminished during the Period for which he shall have been elected, and he shall not receive within that Period any other Emolument from the United States, or any of them.

Before he enter on the Execution of his Office, he shall take the following Oath or Affirmation:—"I do solemnly swear (or affirm) that I will faithfully execute the Office of President of the United States, and will to the best of my Ability, preserve, protect and defend the Constitution of the United States."
Section. 2.

The President shall be Commander in Chief of the Army and Navy of the United States, and of the Militia of the several States, when called into the actual Service of the United States; he may require the Opinion, in writing, of the principal Officer in each of the executive Departments, upon any Subject relating to the Duties of their respective Offices, and he shall have Power to grant Reprieves and Pardons for Offences against the United States, except in Cases of Impeachment.

He shall have Power, by and with the Advice and Consent of the Senate, to make Treaties, provided two thirds of the Senators present concur; and he shall nominate, and by and with the Advice and Consent of the Senate, shall appoint Ambassadors, other public Ministers and Consuls, Judges of the supreme Court, and all other Officers of the United States, whose Appointments are not herein otherwise provided for, and which shall be established by Law: but the Congress may by Law vest the Appointment of such inferior Officers, as they think proper, in the President alone, in the Courts of Law, or in the Heads of Departments.

The President shall have Power to fill up all Vacancies that may happen during the Recess of the Senate, by granting Commissions which shall expire at the End of their next Session.

Section. 3.

He shall from time to time give to the Congress Information of the State of the Union, and recommend to their Consideration such Measures as he shall judge necessary and expedient; he may, on extraordinary Occasions, convene both Houses, or either of them, and in Case of Disagreement between them, with Respect to the Time of Adjournment, he may adjourn them to such Time as he shall think proper; he shall receive Ambassadors and other public Ministers; he shall take Care that the Laws be faithfully executed, and shall Commission all the Officers of the United States.

Section. 4.

The President, Vice President and all civil Officers of the United States, shall be removed from Office on Impeachment for, and Conviction of, Treason, Bribery, or other high Crimes and Misdemeanors.

ARTICLE III.

Section. 1.

The judicial Power of the United States, shall be vested in one supreme Court, and in such inferior Courts as the Congress may from time to time ordain and establish. The Judges, both of the supreme and inferior Courts, shall hold their Offices during good Behaviour, and shall, at stated Times, receive for their Services, a Compensation, which shall not be diminished during their Continuance in Office.

Section. 2.

The judicial Power shall extend to all Cases, in Law and Equity, arising under this Constitution, the Laws of the United States, and Treaties made, or which shall be made, under their Authority;—to all Cases affecting Ambassadors, other public Ministers and Consuls;—to all Cases of admiralty and maritime Jurisdiction;—to Controversies to which the United States shall be a Party;—to Controversies between two or more States;— between a State and Citizens of another State,—between Citizens of different States,—between Citizens of the same State claiming Lands under Grants of different States, and between a State, or the Citizens thereof, and foreign States, Citizens or Subjects.

In all Cases affecting Ambassadors, other public Ministers and Consuls, and those in which a State shall be Party, the supreme Court shall have original Jurisdiction. In all the other Cases before mentioned, the supreme Court shall have appellate Jurisdiction, both as to Law and Fact, with such Exceptions, and under such Regulations as the Congress shall make.

The Trial of all Crimes, except in Cases of Impeachment, shall be by Jury; and such Trial shall be held in the State where the said Crimes shall have been committed; but when not committed within any State, the Trial shall be at such Place or Places as the Congress may by Law have directed.

Section. 3.

Treason against the United States, shall consist only in levying War against them, or in adhering to their Enemies, giving them Aid and Comfort. No Person shall be convicted of Treason unless on the Testimony of two Witnesses to the same overt Act, or on Confession in open Court.

The Congress shall have Power to declare the Punishment of Treason, but no Attainder of Treason shall work Corruption of Blood, or Forfeiture except during the Life of the Person attainted.

ARTICLE. IV.

Section. 1.

Full Faith and Credit shall be given in each State to the public Acts, Records, and judicial Proceedings of every other State. And the Congress may by general Laws prescribe the Manner in which such Acts, Records and Proceedings shall be proved, and the Effect thereof.

Section. 2.

The Citizens of each State shall be entitled to all Privileges and Immunities of Citizens in the several States.

A Person charged in any State with Treason, Felony, or other Crime, who shall flee from Justice, and be found in another State, shall on Demand of the executive Authority of the State from which he fled, be delivered up, to be removed to the State having Jurisdiction of the Crime.

No Person held to Service or Labour in one State, under the Laws thereof, escaping into another, shall, in Consequence of any Law or Regulation therein, be discharged from such Service or

Labour, but shall be delivered up on Claim of the Party to whom such Service or Labour may be due.

Section. 3.

New States may be admitted by the Congress into this Union; but no new State shall be formed or erected within the Jurisdiction of any other State; nor any State be formed by the Junction of two or more States, or Parts of States, without the Consent of the Legislatures of the States concerned as well as of the Congress.

The Congress shall have Power to dispose of and make all needful Rules and Regulations respecting the Territory or other Property belonging to the United States; and nothing in this Constitution shall be so construed as to Prejudice any Claims of the United States, or of any particular State.

Section. 4.

The United States shall guarantee to every State in this Union a Republican Form of Government, and shall protect each of them against Invasion; and on Application of the Legislature, or of the Executive (when the Legislature cannot be convened), against domestic Violence.

ARTICLE. V.

The Congress, whenever two thirds of both Houses shall deem it necessary, shall propose Amendments to this Constitution, or, on the Application of the Legislatures of two thirds of the several States, shall call a Convention for proposing Amendments, which, in either Case, shall be valid to all Intents and Purposes, as Part of this Constitution, when ratified by the Legislatures of three fourths of the several States, or by Conventions in three fourths thereof, as the one or the other Mode of Ratification may be proposed by the Congress; Provided that no Amendment which may be made prior to the Year One thousand eight hundred and eight shall in any Manner affect the first and fourth Clauses in the Ninth Section of the first Article; and that no State, without its Consent, shall be deprived of its equal Suffrage in the Senate.

ARTICLE. VI.

All Debts contracted and Engagements entered into, before the Adoption of this Constitution, shall be as valid against the United States under this Constitution, as under the Confederation.

This Constitution, and the Laws of the United States which shall be made in Pursuance thereof; and all Treaties made, or which shall be made, under the Authority of the United States, shall be the supreme Law of the Land; and the Judges in every State shall be bound thereby, any Thing in the Constitution or Laws of any State to the Contrary notwithstanding.

The Senators and Representatives before mentioned, and the Members of the several State Legislatures, and all executive and judicial Officers, both of the United States and of the several States, shall be bound by Oath or Affirmation, to support this Constitution; but no religious Test shall ever be required as a Qualification to any Office or public Trust under the United States.

ARTICLE. VII.

The Ratification of the Conventions of nine States, shall be sufficient for the Establishment of this Constitution between the States so ratifying the Same.

The Word, "the," being interlined between the seventh and eighth Lines of the first Page, The Word "Thirty" being partly written on an Erazure in the fifteenth Line of the first Page, The Words "is tried" being interlined between the thirty second and thirty third Lines of the first Page and the Word "the" being interlined between the forty third and forty fourth Lines of the second Page.

Attest William Jackson Secretary

done in Convention by the Unanimous Consent of the States present the Seventeenth Day of September in the Year of our Lord one thousand seven hundred and Eighty seven and of the Independance of the United States of America the Twelfth In witness whereof We have hereunto subscribed our Names,

G°. Washington, Presidt and deputy from Virginia

Delaware: Geo: Read, Gunning Bedford jun, John Dickinson, Richard Bassett, Jaco: Broom

Maryland: James McHenry, Dan of St Thos. Jenifer, Danl. Carroll

Virginia: John Blair, James Madison Jr.

North Carolina: Wm. Blount, Richd. Dobbs Spaight, Hu Williamson

South Carolina: J. Rutledge, Charles Cotesworth Pinckney, Charles Pinckney, Pierce Butler

Georgia: William Few, Abr Baldwin

New Hampshire: John Langdon, Nicholas Gilman

Massachusetts: Nathaniel Gorham, Rufus King

Connecticut: Wm. Saml. Johnson, Roger Sherman

New York: Alexander Hamilton

New Jersey: Wil: Livingston, David Brearley, Wm. Paterson, Jona: Dayton

Pensylvania: B Franklin, Thomas Mifflin, Robt. Morris, Geo. Clymer, Thos. FitzSimons, Jared Ingersoll, James Wilson, Gouv Morris

Index